WINNING CASINO PLAY

ABOUT THE AUTHOR

Avery Cardoza is the foremost gambling authority in the world and best-selling author of twenty-one gambling books and advanced strategies, including *How to Win at Gambling*, *Secrets of Winning Slots*, and the classic, *Winning Casino Blackjack for the Non-Counter*.

Cardoza began his gambling career underage in Las Vegas as a professional blackjack player beating the casinos at their own game and was soon barred from one casino after another. In 1981, when even the biggest casinos refused him play, Cardoza founded Cardoza Publishing, which has sold more than five million books and published close to 100 gaming titles.

Though originally from Brooklyn, New York, where he is occasionally found, Cardoza has used his winnings to pursue a lifestyle of extensive traveling in exotic locales around the world.

In 1994, he established Cardoza Entertainment, a multimedia development and publishing house, to produce interactive gambling simulations that give players a taste of a real casino with animated and responsive dealers, and the full scale of bets at the correct odds. The result, *Avery Cardoza's Casino*, featuring 65 gambling variations, became an instant entertainment hit making its way onto USA Today's best-seller's list. It also catapulted Cardoza Entertainment, measured by average sales per title, as the number two seller of games in the entire industry for the first six months of 1997, ahead of such giants as Dreamworks, Microsoft, and others. Their second title, *Avery Cardoza's 100 Slots*, was a simulated slots palace with 101 machines, and became another best-seller.

Cardoza Entertainment's (www.cardozaent.com) activities in developing an online casino (www.cardozacasino.com) for real money has attracted worldwide interest in the online gambling community. As the highest profile player in casino simulations, and the only publisher featuring actual simulations with true odds and interactive animated dealers, Cardoza Entertainment is acknowledged as the leading player in the online casino market.

WINNING CASINO PLAY

Avery Cardoza

Cardoza Publishing

First Edition

First Printing	May 1994
Second Printing	September 1995

New, Second Edition

First Printing	April 1999
Second Printing	February 2000

Library of Congress Catalog Card Number: 98-74285
ISBN: 1-58042-012-5

Write for your free catalogue of gambling books,
advanced and computer strategies.

CARDOZA PUBLISHING
PO Box 1500 Cooper Station, New York, NY 10276
Phone (718)743-5229 • Fax (718)743-8284

E-Mail: cardozapub@aol.com
www.cardozapub.com

TABLE OF CONTENTS

INTRODUCTION   **9**

CASINO BASICS   **11**

MONEY MANAGEMENT   **15**

WINNING AT BLACKJACK   **21**

Introduction	21
Beginner's Guide to Casino Blackjack	22
Rules and Variations of the Casino Centers	40
The Optimal Basics Strategies	45
Master Charts	68
Single and Multiple Deck Differences	72
Player's Options	74
Winning Strategies	76

WINNING AT CRAPS — 81

Introduction — 81
Beginner's Guide to Casino Craps — 82
Understanding the Odds — 95
The Best Bets — 101
The Rest of the Bets — 124
Winning Strategies: Betting With the Dice — 137
Winning Strategies: Betting Agaisnt The Dice — 141

WINNING AT ROULETTE — 146

Introduction — 146
The Basics of Roulette — 147
The Bets — 156
Winning Strategies — 165

WINNING AT SLOTS — 177

Introduction — 177
The Slots Setting — 179
The Elements of a Slot Machine — 181
The Play Buttons — 185
The Displays — 188
The Basics of Play — 190
Types of Machines — 197
Slot Clubs — 204
Slot Percentages — 208
Winning Strategies — 209

WINNING AT VIDEO POKER 212

Introduction	212
Player Advantage in Video Poker	213
Types of Machines	214
How to Play	215
Winning Strategies	227

WINNING AT CARIBBEAN STUD POKER 238

Introduction	238
The Basics of Caribbean Stud Poker	239
The Play of the Game	246
The Maximum Bonus Payout	252
The Progressive Jackpot	254
House Percentage	259
Winning Strategies	262
Progressive $1 Bet Strategy	267
Betting Strategy	269
Overall Winning Strategy	269

WINNING AT LET IT RIDE 272

Introduction	272
Beginner's Guide to Let it Ride	273
The Winning Poker Hands	278
The Play of the Game	280
$1 Bonus or Tournament Bet	286
Let it Ride Bonus	287
Let it Ride Tournament Bet	292
The Winning Strategies	297
The New Models	305
Odds of Drawing Hands	311
Strategy Overview	313

INTRODUCTION

You can win money at gambling! Beating the casinos at their own game is fun, a lot of fun, however, winning is a skill that must be learned. And that's what we're here to do. In this book, I'll show you all the basics you need to gamble intelligently, and how to come home a winner!

We look at all the major casino games you'll find – blackjack, craps, video poker, slots, roulette, Caribbean stud poker, and let it ride – and show you how to play and win money at each one of them. To make sure you have a fair shot at bringing home the bacon, we also cover the all-important money management skills, skills necessary for a winner to know and use properly.

There are lots of charts and sane advice to help you win. For each game, we go over the winning concepts carefully so that you're fully conversant with the skills necessary to come out ahead while having fun at the tables.

In *blackjack*, you can enjoy a mathematical

advantage, and we'll show you how to beat single and multiple deck games; in *craps*, you'll learn how to make the best bets so that the majority of your money goes on wagers the house has no edge on; in *video poker*, we'll show the best machines to play and how to actually have the edge; in *roulette*, you'll learn how best to play the 150 possible wagers; and in *slots*, you'll find out how to improve your chances for the big jackpot!

Additionally, in this new edition updated for the millennium, we've added the playing strategies for the two relative newcomers to the casino floor, Caribbean stud poker and let it ride, and expanded the rest of the book, particularly the slots chapter, to reflect the many new aspects of that game.

All the winning information you need to get started is here in this book, so read on.

Let's beat the casino!

CASINO BASICS

INTRODUCTION

The thrill of gambling, and especially winning, has kept casinos flush with players trying their skills and luck at the games offered. While some players win, and some lose, all players find their hearts beating ever so harder as money laid on the line awaits the laws of almighty chance.

In this section, we'll go over the essentials of playing in a casino - how to deal with changing money and making bets, the currencies used by the casinos, how to get free drinks and cigarettes, what's involved in tipping, and some other basics of the casino setting.

CONVERTING TRAVELLER'S CHECKS AND MONEY ORDERS TO CASH

The dealers accept only cash or chips at the table, so if you bring traveller's checks, money order or the like, you must go to the area of the casino marked **Casino Cashier** to get these converted to cash. Bring proper identification to insure a smooth transaction.

CASINO CHIPS

Chip denominations run in $1, $5, $25, $100 and $500 units. If you're a big stakes player, you may find $1,000, $2,500, $5,000 and $10,000 chips available!

The usual color scheme is as follows: $1 chips are either silver dollars (as used to be standard in all the Vegas casinos) or blue chips or other color, $5 chips are red, $25 are green, and $100 are black. In casinos, $1 chips are called *silver*, $5 chips as *nickels*, $25 chips as *quarters*, and $100 chips as *dollars*. Unless playing at a 25¢ minimum table, dollar units are the minimum chip available. When stakes are under $1 per bet, as in special games or slot machines, standard coins such as quarters, will be used.

BETTING

Casinos prefer that the player uses chips for betting purposes, for the handling of money at the tables is cumbersome and slows the game.

Though bets can be made with cash, all payoffs will be in chips.

HOUSE LIMITS

The house limits will be posted on placards located on each corner of the table. They indicate the minimum bet required and the maximum bet allowed.

Minimum bets range from $1 and $5 per bet, to a maximum of $500, $1000 or $2,000 a bet. Occasionally, 25¢ tables may be found as well, but don't count on it. If special arrangements are made, a player can bet as much as he can muster in certain casinos.

In 1981, a man placed a bet for $777,777 at the Horseshoe Casino in Las Vegas. He bet the don't pass in craps, and walked out two rolls later with one and a half million dollars in cash!

CONVERTING CHIPS INTO CASH

Dealers do not convert your chips into cash. Once you've bought your chips at the table, that cash is dropped into a dropbox, and thereafter is unobtainable. When you are ready to convert your chips back to cash, take them to the cashier's cage where the transaction will be done.

FREE DRINKS AND CIGARETTES

Casinos offer their customers unlimited free drinking while gambling at the tables or slot machines. In addition to alcoholic beverages, a player can order milk, soft drinks, juices or any other beverages available. These are served by a cocktail waitress.

Cigarettes and cigars are also complimentary and can be ordered through the same cocktail waitress.

TIPPING

Tipping, or **toking**, as it is called in casino parlance, is totally at your discretion, and in no way should be considered an obligation.

If you toke, toke only when you're winning, and only if the crew is friendly and helpful to you. Do not toke dealers that you don't like or ones that try to make you feel guilty about not tipping. Dealers that make playing an unpleasant experience for you deserve nothing.

MONEY MANAGEMENT

INTRODUCTION

Winning at gambling requires not only the playing of the correct strategies but also the intelligent use of one's monetary resources. Preparation is key.

To emerge a winner from the streaky swings of fortune inherent in gambling takes a certain degree of emotional control, for the temptation to ride a winning streak too hard in the hopes of a big killing or to bet wildly during a losing streak, trying for a quick comeback, can spell doom.

Big winning sessions can dissipate into small wins or even disastrous losses while moderately bad losing sessions can turn into a nightmare.

Money management is the most important factor in the winning formula, so don't gloss over this section. Without these skills, you cannot win at gambling, even though the odds may favor you. So give this section a good read, and take our advice seriously.

If you do, you'll find yourself on the money end of the table, as a winner, and that's what our goal in gambling is all about!

Money management skills can be divided into the following three categories:

> • **Emotional Control**
> • **Bankrolling**
>   (total bankroll, table bankroll)
> • **When to Quit**
>   (maximize gains, minimize losses)

Before we look at these skills more closely, there's one extremely important point that must be thoroughly understood.

Never gamble with money you cannot afford to lose either financially or emotionally.

Betting with money you cannot afford to lose adversely affects decision making. Rather than playing your best game, your strategy gets restricted to the confines of your monetary or emotional situation, rather than your intelligence and skill.

MONEY MANAGEMENT

Betting with "scared money" is a guaranteed way to ensure yourself a losing career as a gambler.

EMOTIONAL CONTROL

It is important to recognize that the ups and downs of your moods and feelings affect the quality of your play. A tired player, or an upset player, won't play with a clear head and will make mistakes or unwise decisions that cost money.

But don't let that happen to you. Basically, whenever you feel emotionally unprepared to risk money, it's time to take a break. And if, for whatever reason, the game becomes a cause of anxiety and ceases to be entertainment, than it's time to take a breather.

Play again later on, when you're more alert and confident. Remember, the casinos aren't going anywhere. There's lots of time to get your bets down.

For gambling to be a pleasurable and successful experience every time you sit down at the tables, you must feel like gambling and must be able to afford possible losses, emotionally as well as financially.

Bottom line, gambling wisely should give you emotional satisfaction, not take it away.

BANKROLL YOURSELF PROPERLY

To be a successful player, your bankroll must be large enough to withstand the normal ups and downs that are the very nature of gambling. Under-capitalization and overbetting are dangerous for two reasons.

First, a normal downward trend can wipe out a limited money supply. Second, and more important, a player feeling pressured by limited capital will play less intelligently than smart play dictates. And that is where you start giving the odds back to the casino and begin playing like a loser.

The key to winning is to play for the win and that means smart money management - using your head. If the amount staked on a bet is over your level, you're playing in the wrong game. Play only at levels of betting you're comfortable with.

MINIMIZING LOSSES

Here are three simple guidelines that, if followed, will save you a lot of money.

• **Limit Your Table Losses**. Do not dig in for more money, and you can never be a big loser. As they say, the first loss is the cheapest. Take a break, try again later. You never want go get into a position where losing so much in one session totally demoralizes you.

• **Never Increase Your Bets Beyond Your Bankroll Range**. In other words, always bet within your means.

• **Never Increase Your Bet Size To Catch Up And Break Even**. Raising your bets will not change the odds of the game, nor will it change your luck. What it will do is make your chances of taking a terrible beating frighteningly high. As we discussed earlier do not get into a position where losing so much in one session destroys any reasonable chance of coming out even. You can't win all the time. Rest awhile; you'll get 'em later.

WHEN TO QUIT - MAXIMIZING GAINS

What often separates the winners from the losers is - the winners, when winning, leave the table a winner, and when losing, restrict their losses to affordable amounts. Smart gamblers never allow themselves to get destroyed at the table.

As a player, you have one big advantage that, if used properly, will insure you success as a gambler - You can quit playing whenever you want to. To come out ahead, you must minimize your losses when you lose and maximize your gains when you win. This way, winning sessions will eclipse losing sessions and overall, you'll come out a winner!

Let's move on now to the games themselves!

WINNING AT BLACKJACK

INTRODUCTION

Blackjack turned into the most popular casino game when the word got out - that it can be beaten! With proper play, you can actually have the edge over the casino, and thus, the expectation to win money every time you play!

We cover the fundamentals of casino blackjack here - the rules of the game, the players' options, the variations offered in casinos, how to bet, casino jargon, how to play and everything else you'll need to know about playing winning casino blackjack.

BEGINNER'S GUIDE TO CASINO BLACKJACK

Blackjack Table and Layout

Blackjack, or **21** as the game is often called, is played at a curved oval table, with room for five to seven players. The players sit in chairs (or they can stand) around the curved portion of the table, with the dealer on the flat side, standing and facing the players.

On the printed layout, there are corresponding betting spots, usually rectangular, for each participating player. It is here where bets are placed and the cards are dealt. There will also be several of the rules printed on the surface. You'll often see, *Insurance Pays 2 to 1*, *Dealer Must Draw to 16 and Stand on All 17s* and *Blackjack Pays 3 to 2*.

We'll go into these rules in a moment, but first, let's take a look at the illustration of the blackjack layout on the following page.

The Blackjack Layout

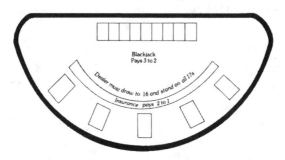

The Decks of Cards

Nevada casinos use one, two, four, six and sometimes as many as eight decks of cards in their blackjack games. Often, within the same casino, single and multiple deck games will be offered.

Typically though, outside of Nevada, multiple deck blackjack dealt out of a shoe is the standard of play in the world whether played in Atlantic City, on casino boats, in Indian casinos or anywhere else blackjack may be found.

When one or two decks are used, the dealer holds the cards in his hand. When more than two decks are used, the cards are dealt from a rectangular plastic or wooden device known as a **shoe**.

The shoe is designed to hold multiple decks of cards, and allows the cards to be easily removed one at a time by the dealer.

Each deck used in blackjack is a standard pack of 52 cards, consisting of 4 cards of each value, Ace through King. Suits have no relevance in blackjack. Only the numerical value of the cards count.

Card Values

Each card is counted at face value. 2=2 points, 3=3 points, 10=10 points, while the face cards, Jack, Queen and King, are counted as 10 points. The Ace can be counted as 1 point or 11 points at the player's discretion. When the Ace is counted as 11 points, that hand is called **soft**, as in the hand Ace, 7 = *soft 18*. All other totals, including hands where the Ace counts as 1 point, are called hard, as in the hand 10, 6, A = *hard 17*.

The dealer must count his Ace as 11 if that gives him a hand totaling 17 to 21, otherwise he must count the Ace as 1 point.

In some casinos the rules dictate that the dealer must draw on soft 17. In these casinos, the dealer's Ace will count as 1 point when combined with cards totalling 6 points, and the dealer will have to draw until he forms a hand of at least hard 17.

Casino Personnel

The casino employee responsible for the running of the blackjack game is called the **dealer**. The dealer's duties are to deal the cards to the players, and play out his own hand according to the rules of the game. He converts money into chips for players entering the game or buying in for more chips during the course of the game, makes the correct payoffs for winning hands, and collects bets from the losers.

The dealer's supervisor - technically called the **floorman**, but more commonly referred to as the **pit boss** - is responsible for the supervision of between 4-6 tables. He makes sure the games are run smoothly and he settles any disputes that may arise with a player. More importantly, his job is to oversee the exchange of money and to correct any errors that may occur.

Entering a Game

To enter a blackjack game, sit down at any unoccupied seat at the blackjack table, place the money you wish to gamble with near the betting box in front of you and inform the dealer that you would like to get some chips for your cash. Chips may be purchased in various denominations. Let the dealer know which chips or combination of chips you'd like.

The dealer will take your money and call out the amount he is changing so that the pit boss is aware that a transaction is taking place and can supervise that exchange.

Object of the Game

The player's object in casino blackjack is to beat the dealer. This can be achieved in two ways:

• When the player has a higher total than the dealer without exceeding 21.

• When the dealer's total exceeds 21 (assuming the player has not exceeded 21 first).

In casino blackjack, as opposed to private games, if the player and the dealer both hold the same total of 21 or less, the hand is a **push**, nobody wins.

WINNING AT BLACKJACK

Busting or Breaking - Automatic Losers

If the drawing of additional cards to the initial two cards dealt causes the point total to exceed 21, then that hand is said to be **busted**, an automatic loss. Busted hands should be turned up immediately. Once the player has busted, his hand is lost, even if the dealer busts as well afterwards. If the dealer busts, all remaining players automatically win their bets.

Blackjack - Automatic Winner

If the original two card hand contains an Ace with any 10 or face card (J,Q,K), the hand is called a **blackjack**, or **natural**, and is an automatic winner for the player whose bet is paid off at 3-2. Blackjacks should be turned up immediately. If the dealer gets a blackjack, all players lose their bets. (The dealer wins only the player's bet, not the 3-2 payoff the player would receive.)

If both the dealer and the player are dealt a blackjack, the hand is a push.

Payoffs

All bets are paid off at even money ($5 bet wins $5), except in cases where the player receives a blackjack which is a 3 to 2 payoff ($5 bet wins $7.50) or when the player exercises an option that allows him to double his bet. In these instances (doubling and splitting), the payoff is equal to the new doubled bet. If a bet is doubled from $5 to $10, a win would pay off $10.

Single Vs. Multiple Deck Basics

In single and double deck games, the player is dealt his cards face down and gets to physically hold them.

In a game of four or more decks, the cards will be dealt out of a shoe (as opposed to hand-held as in the one or two deck games), and the player is not supposed to touch them at any time. Instead, playing decisions are indicated by hand signals.

Dealer's Rules

The dealer must play by prescribed guidelines. He must draw to any hand 16 or below and stand on any total 17-21. As mentioned above, some casinos require the dealer to draw on soft 17. The dealer has no options and cannot deviate from these rules.

Player's Options

Unlike the dealer, the player can vary his strategy. After receiving his first two cards the player has the following options:

Drawing (Hitting)

If the player is not satisfied with his two card total he can draw additional cards. To draw a card, the player scrapes the felt surface with his cards, scraping toward his body. In a game where both the player's cards are dealt face up, the player is not supposed to touch the cards and instead scratches the felt with his index finger or points toward the cards if he desires additional cards.

Single Deck Hitting and Standing

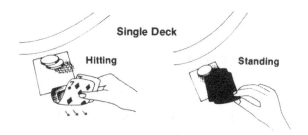

Standing

When a player is satisfied with his original two cards, and doesn't wish to draw additional cards, he signals this by sliding his cards face down under his bet. When the cards are dealt face up, the player indicates his decision to stand by waving his hand palm down over his cards.

Multiple Deck Hitting and Standing

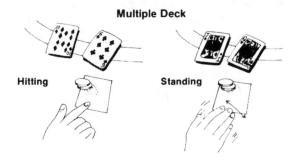

Doubling Down

This option allows the player to double his original bet, in which case he must draw one additional card to his hand and cannot draw any additional cards thereafter. To double down, the player turns his cards face up, and places them in front of his bet. Then he takes an amount equal to his original bet and places those chips next to that bet, so that there are now two equivalent bets side by side.

In games where the cards are dealt face up, the player simply places the additional bet next to his original to indicate the double down.

The dealer will then deal one card face down, usually slipping that card under the player's bet. The bettor may look at that card if he desires.

Splitting Pairs

If dealt a pair of identical value cards, such as 3-3, 7-7, 8-8 (any combination of 10, J, Q, K is considered a pair), the player can split these cards so that two separate hands are formed. To split a pair, the player turns the pair face up, separates them, putting each card in its own place in front of his bet. He then places a bet equal to the original wager behind the second hand. Each hand is played separately, using finger and hand signals to indicate hitting and standing.

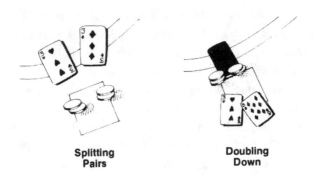

Splitting
Pairs

Doubling
Down

Splitting Pairs and Doubling Down

In games where both player cards are dealt face up, the split is indicated by placing the additional bet next to the original one, and after, using hand signals as above to indicate hitting or standing.

If the first card dealt to either split hand has a value identical to the original split cards, that card may be split again (resplit) into a third hand, with the exception of Aces. When the player splits Aces, he can receive only one card on each Ace and may not draw again, no matter what card is drawn.

Doubling Down After Splitting

The player can double down on one or both of the hands resulting from a split according to the normal doubling rules of the casino. This option is offered in all Atlantic City casinos and in certain Nevada casinos.

For example, if a pair of 8s are split, and a 3 is drawn to the first 8 for an 11, the player may elect to double down on that 11. He does so by placing an amount equal to the original bet next to the 11, and receives only one additional card for that hand. The other 8 is played separately and can be doubled as well should an advantageous card such as a 2 or 3 be drawn.

Since options allowed are often in flux, sometimes changing from one month to the next, when playing, check to see if this advantageous option is available.

Surrender (Late Surrender)

The player may "surrender" his original two card hand and forfeit one half of his bet *after* it has been determined that the dealer does not have a blackjack and before the player has exercised any of his other options. Surrender is offered in only a few casinos.

To surrender, the bettor turns and places both his cards face up in front of his bet, and says "surrender," or in a game where both player cards are dealt face up, he announces his intention verbally to the dealer. The dealer will collect the cards and take one half of the bet.

Early Surrender

A player option to give up his hand and lose half his bet *before* the dealer checks for a blackjack. This very favorable option was originally introduced in Atlantic City but is no longer offered because of changes in Atlantic City rules.

Insurance

If the dealer shows an Ace as his upcard, he will ask the players if they want insurance. If any player exercises this option, he is in effect betting that the dealer has a 10-value card as his hole card, a blackjack. To take insurance, the player places up to one-half the amount of his bet in the area marked "insurance."

If the dealer does indeed have a blackjack, he gets paid 2 to 1 on the insurance bet, while losing the original bet. In effect, the transaction is a "standoff," and no money is lost. If the dealer does not have a blackjack, the insurance bet is lost and play continues.

If the player holds a blackjack and takes insurance on the dealer's Ace, the payoff will be even-money whether the dealer has a blackjack or not. Suppose the player has a $10 bet and takes insurance for $5 on his blackjack. If the dealer has a blackjack, the player wins 2 to 1 on his $5 insurance bet and ties with his own blackjack. If the dealer doesn't have a blackjack, the player loses the $5 insurance bet but gets paid 3 to 2 on his blackjack. Either way the bettor wins $10.

Insurance Strategy

Insurance is a bad bet for the following reason:

Making an insurance wager is betting that the dealer has a 10 under his Ace. Since the insurance payoff is 2 to 1, the wager will only be a profitable option for the player when the ratio of 10s to other cards is either equal to or less than 2 to 1.

A full deck has 36 non-tens and 16 tens, a ratio greater than 2 to 1. If the first deal off the top of the deck gives us a hand of 9,7, and the dealer shows an Ace, then we know three cards, all non-tens. Now the ratio is 33 to 16, still greater than 2 to 1, still a poor bet. If you have two 10s for a 20, then the ratio is 35 to 14, making insurance a more costly proposition.

In a multiple deck game, taking insurance is even a worse bet than in a single deck one.

Insuring a Blackjack

Taking insurance when you have a blackjack is also a bad bet, despite the well-intentioned advice of dealers and other players to always "insure" a blackjack. When you have a blackjack, you know three cards, your 10 and Ace, and the dealer's Ace. The already poor starting ratio of 36 tens to 16 non-tens gets worse, becoming 34 to 15 in a single deck game.

Taking insurance when you have a blackjack in a single deck game, gives the house an 8% advantage, a poor proposition for the player.

The Play of the Game

The dealer begins by shuffling the cards and offering the cut to one of the players. If refused, it is offered to another player. The dealer then completes the cut, and removes the top card, called the **burn card**. In single and double deck games, the burn card is either put under the deck face up, where all subsequent cards will be placed, or is put face down into a plastic case (procedures vary from casino to casino) to be followed similarly by future discards.

In games dealt out of a shoe, the burn card will be placed most of the way into the shoe and discards will be put in the plastic case.

Players must make their bets before the cards are dealt.

The dealer deals clockwise from his left to his right, one card at a time, until each player and the dealer have received two cards. The players cards are usually dealt face down in a single or double deck game, though it makes no difference if they are dealt face up as they usually are in a game dealt out of a shoe, for the dealer is bound by strict rules from which he cannot deviate.

The dealer deals only one of his two cards face up. This card is called an **upcard**. The face down card is known as the **hole card** or the **downcard**.

If the dealer's upcard is an Ace, he will ask the players if they want insurance. Players that decide to take that option may bet up to one-half their wager in front of their bet in the area marked insurance.

If the dealer has a blackjack, all players that did not take insurance lose their original bets unless a player holds a blackjack also - where it's a push. Players that took insurance break even on the play. If the dealer doesn't have a blackjack, he collects the lost insurance bets and play continues.

Play begins with the bettor on the dealer's left, in the position known as **first base**.

This player has the option to stand, hit, double down, split (if he has two cards of equal value) or surrender (if allowed). A player may draw cards until he is satisfied with his total or busts, or he may exercise one of the other options discussed earlier.

Play then moves to the next player. If any player busts (goes over 21) or receives a blackjack, he must turn over his cards immediately. If a bust, the dealer will collect the lost bet. If a blackjack, the dealer will pay the player 3 to 2 on his bet.

After the last player has acted upon his cards, the dealer will turn his hole card over so that all players can view both of his cards. He must play his hand according to the strict guidelines regulating his play; drawing to 17, then standing. (In some casinos the dealer must draw to a soft 17.) If the dealer busts, all players still in the game for that round of play win automatically.

After playing his hand, the dealer will turn over each player's cards in turn, paying the winners, and collecting from the losers. Once the bettor has played his hand, he shouldn't touch his cards again. He should let the dealer expose his hand which he will do when he has played out his own hand.

In a game dealt from a shoe (four or more decks), the player should never touch the cards anyway.

When the round has been completed, all players must place a new bet before the next deal.

Tipping

The best way to tip a dealer is to place a bet for the dealer in front of your own bet, so that his chances of winning that toke are tied up with your hand. If the hand is won, you both win together; if the hand is lost, you lose together.

By being partners on the hand, you establish camaraderie with the dealer. Naturally, he or she will be rooting for you to win. This is the best way to tip, for when you win, the dealer wins double - the tip amount you bet plus the winnings from that bet.

RULES AND VARIATIONS OF THE CASINO CENTERS

Blackjack games are basically the same wherever played, though the rules and variations vary from casino center to casino center, and sometimes, they even differ within a casino itself. However, the strategies we'll show you will arm you for any game, and give you the tools to be a winner no matter the variation.

The standard casino game is the same no matter where you play blackjack.

Following are the main changes you'll find from one game to another, all of them being relatively minor. The first condition favors the player, the second condition favors the casino, and thus is disadvantageous to the player.

• Dealer stands on all 17s vs. dealer hits on soft 17

• Single deck vs. multiple deck (2, 4, 6 or 8 decks)

• Doubling down on any initial two card combination vs. doubling down restricted to certain totals, such as 10 and 11 only.

• Doubling after splitting allowed vs. not allowed.

Nevada Rules

The Las Vegas Strip rules are advantageous to the player and gives one a slight edge on the single deck game if our strategies are followed.

The rule exceptions noted in Downtown Las Vegas and in Northern Nevada games are slightly disadvantageous to the player, but these can easily be overcome by using the winning techniques presented later.

Las Vegas Strip Rules

• Dealer must draw on all totals of 16 or less, and stand on all totals of 17-21.

• Player may take insurance on a dealer's Ace.

• Insurance payoffs are 2 to 1.

• Player receives a 3 to 2 payoff on his blackjack.

• Player may double down on any initial two card combination.

• Identical pairs may be split, resplit, and drawn to as desired with the exception of split Aces, on which the player is allowed only one hit on each Ace.

• One, two, four and bigger deck games are standard.

Downtown Las Vegas Rules

Rules and condition are the same as the Las Vegas Strip rules with one exception:

• Dealer must draw to soft 17.

Northern Nevada Rules

Same as Las Vegas Strip rules with two exceptions:

• Dealer must draw to soft 17.

• Doubling is restricted to two card totals of 10 and 11 only.

Atlantic City Rules

To protect against collusion between the player and the dealer, the dealer does not check his hole card for a blackjack (as is standard in Nevada) until all players have finished playing out their hands.

This safeguard does not affect the player's chances of winning, for if the dealer does indeed have a blackjack, any additional money the player may have wagered on a doubled or split hand will be returned. Only the original bet is lost. The standard rules are:

- Dealer must draw to all totals 16 or less, and stand on all totals of 17-21.
- Player may take insurance on a dealer's Ace.
- Insurance payoffs are 2 to 1.
- Player receives a 3 to 2 payoff on his blackjack.
- Player may double on any initial two card combination.
- Identical pairs may be split but not resplit.
- Doubling after splitting allowed.
- Four, six and eight decks are standard.

European Rules

Blackjack is offered in numerous countries around Europe with the rules and variations changing slightly from place to place. However, the following conditions apply in a good many of these places.

- Dealer must draw to all totals 16 or less,and stand on all totals of 17-21.
- Player may take insurance on a dealer's Ace.

- Insurance payoffs are 2 to 1.
- Player receives a 3 to 2 payoff on his black-jack.
- Doubling Down on 9-11 Only.
- Standees Permitted.
- No Hole Card Rule.
- 4-6 Decks Standard.
- If player draws a 2 on a A8 double down hand, total counts as 11, not 21.

RULES AROUND THE WORLD
Bahamas • Caribbean • Europe • Southern Africa • Asia • South America • Other Locations

The general blackjack variations we presented under the European Rules are the most prevalent style of play you'll find in casinos around the world. However, you'll find variations from country to country. For example, in Asian and Caribbean casinos, surrender is often allowed. In Great Britain, many European casinos, southern Africa and other locales, you may find doubling after splitting permitted.

In any case, always find out the particular rules of a game before playing so you know what you're up against and how best to play your hands.

However, no matter where you play, the game of blackjack is basically the same give or take the minor options discussed, and we'll show you how to win against any variation.

(Note that single deck blackjack is hard to find or nonexistent outside the Nevada casinos. Multiple deck blackjack is the predominant style of play in casinos around the world.)

THE OPTIMAL BASIC STRATEGIES
The Ten Factor

The most striking feature of blackjack is the dominant role that the 10 value cards (10, J, Q, K) play - what we call the **ten factor**.

Collectively, the 10s constitute just under 1/3 of the deck (16 out of 52 cards). Because the 10s are such a dominant factor in a deck of cards, it's correct to think of the dealer's hand as *gravitating* toward a total 10 points greater than his exposed upcard.

Thus, for example, starting out with an upcard of 9, the dealer will make a hand of 19 about 36% of the time and 19 or better 52% of the time.

The Dealer Rules & the Ten Factor

Our strategy is based on the fact that the dealer must play by prescribed guidelines from which he cannot deviate. He must draw to all totals 16 or below, and stand on all totals 17-21 (except in casinos that require the dealer to draw to soft 17). All hard totals that exceed hard 21 are automatic dealer losses.

Our knowledge of the 10 factor and the dealer's rules allows us to separate the dealer's upcards into two distinct groupings: 2s through 6s, the dealer *stiff cards*, and 7s through As (Aces), the dealer *pat cards*.

We'll base our strategies accordingly.

The high concentration of 10 value cards in the deck tells us that the dealer has a good chance of busting when his upcard is a 2, 3, 4, 5 or 6, a *stiff card*, and that there is an excellent chance he will make his hand when showing the *pat cards*, the 7, 8, 9, 10, A. Even when he hasn't a 10 in the hole, combinations such as 89, A7, 99 and so forth, give him an automatic pat hand as well.

General Principles

1. When the dealer shows a 7, 8, 9, 10 or A, hit all hard totals of 16 or below (unless doubling or splitting is more profitable - in any case, you will always draw a card).

2. When the dealer shows a 2, 3, 4, 5 or 6, stand on all hard totals of 12 or more. Do not bust against a dealer stiff card. Exception - Hit 12 vs. 2, 3.

Player Hand of 11 or Less: (Hard Totals)

Always draw to any hard total 11 or less (unless a doubling or splitting option is more profitable). There is no risk of busting, no matter what is drawn, while the drawing of a card can only strengthen our hand.

Player Hand of 17-21: (Hard Totals)

Always stand on these hard totals (17-21), for the risk of busting is too high to make drawing worthwhile.

Player Hand of 12-16: (Hard Totals)

With these hands, our play is not an obvious draw such as the 11 or less grouping for the risk of drawing a 10 or other high card and busting is substantial. Our hand is not an obvious stand decision either such as the 17-21 grouping, for the only times we will win with these weak totals of 12-16 are the times that the dealer busts.

It is when we hold hard totals 12-16 (stiffs) that the player's big disadvantage of having to go first (the only built-in house advantage) is a costly proposition. If we draw to hard totals and bust, we are automatic losers. But, on the other hand, if we stand, we will win with these weak totals only when the dealer busts.

It is important to realize that the decision to hit or stand with hard totals 12-16 is a strategy of minimizing losses, for no matter what we do, we have a potentially losing hand against any dealer upcard. Do not expect to win when you hold a stiff.

However, in order to maximize the gain from our overall strategy, we must minimize the losses in disadvantageous situations (as above), and maximize our gains in advantageous ones.

Player Hands 12-16 vs. Dealer Pat Cards 7-Ace

When the dealer's upcard is a 7 through an Ace, you should expect the dealer to make his hand, for he will bust only about one time in four, a mere 25% of the time. If we stand on our hard totals 12-16, we will win only the times that the dealer busts.

You will bust often when drawing to your stiffs, but do not let that dissuade you form hitting your stiffs against pat cards. The strategy on these plays is to minimize losses. We cannot afford to stand and sacrifice our bet to the 3 out of 4 hands that the dealer will make.

When the dealer shows a 7, 8, 9, 10, or Ace, hit all hard totals 16 or below.

Player Hands of 12-16 vs. Dealer Pat Cards 2-6

The greater busting potential of the dealer stiff cards makes standing with hard player totals of 12-16 a big gain over drawing. While we will win only 40% of these hands (the times that the dealer busts), standing is a far superior strategy to drawing, for we will bust too often drawing to our own stiffs against upcards that will bust fairly often themselves.

The times that we would make pat totals by drawing wouldn't guarantee us winners either, for the dealer will often make equal or better totals.

On these plays, our disadvantage of having to go first makes drawing too costly, for once we bust, we automatically lose. Though the dealer will make more hands than bust, our strategy here is to minimize losses so that when we get our good hands, we'll come out an overall winner.

Exception - Hit Player 12 vs. 2, 3

Hitting 12 vs. 2, 3 is the only basic strategy exception to drawing with a stiff total against a dealer's stiff upcard. The double bust factor is not as costly on these plays, for only the 10s will bust our 12. Similarly, the dealer will bust less often showing a 2 or a 3 than with the other stiff cards, 4, 5 and 6.

HITTING AND STANDING - SOFT TOTALS

Player Hand of A2, A3, A4, A5

Unless the player is able to double down, he should always draw a card to these hands. Standing is a poor option, for these totals will win only when the dealer busts. The player has nothing to lose by drawing (no draw can bust these totals), and may improve his total. Players that stand on these hands might just as well give the casinos their money.

Draw on A2-A5 against all dealer upcards.

For soft totals A6 - A9, we want to know:

• What are our chances of winning by standing?

• What are the chances of improving our hand by drawing additional cards?

Player Hand of Soft 17 (A6)

Always draw on soft 17 no matter what the dealer shows as an upcard. (In Las Vegas and Atlantic City and other locations where allowed, the correct strategy may be to double down. See doubling section.) This standing total is so weak that attempting to improve our hand by drawing is always a tremendous gain against any upcard.

When a casino requires the dealer to draw to soft 17, it is a disadvantageous rule to the player. Though the dealer will sometimes bust by drawing to a soft 17, in the long run he will make more powerful totals and have more winners. It affects the player the same way.

Player Hand of Soft 18

Against dealer stiff totals of 2, 3, 4, 5 and 6, standing with our 18 is a smart strategy move (unless playing Las Vegas or Atlantic City doubling rules where doubling will often be a big player gain). We have a strong total against these weak dealer upcards.

Stand against dealer upcards of 7 and 8, for our 18 is a solid hand. Against the 7, we have a winning total, and against the 8, we figure to have a potential push, as these dealer upcards gravitate toward 17 and 18 respectively. We do not want to risk our strong position by drawing.

Against the powerful dealer upcards of 9, 10, Ace, our standing total of 18 is a potentially losing hand and thus we try to improve it. Soft 18 is only a fair total and by drawing we are not chancing a powerful total but rather attempting to improve a weak situation.

As a matter of fact, for every 100 plays (at $1 a play) that we draw rather than stand on soft 18 vs. 9 and 10, we will gain $9 and $4 respectively. You must realize that 18 vs. 9, 10, Ace is not a winning hand and since our 18 is a soft total, we have a chance to minimize losses by drawing.

Player Hand of Soft 19 and 20

These hands are strong player totals as they stand. Do not draw any cards. We have no need of improving these already powerful totals.

Doubling Down

Doubling down is valuable option for it gives the player a chance to double his bet in advantageous situations.

One of the most important factors to consider when contemplating the doubling option is the 10 factor - we are more likely to draw a 10 on our double than any other card value. Thus, doubling on a total of 11, where the drawing of a 10 gives us an unbeatable 21, is a more powerful double than an initial two card total of 9, where the drawing of 10 gives us a strong total of 19, not as powerful as the 21.

On the other hand, we would not double any hand of hard 12 or more, for the drawing of a 10 would bust our total, and we would have an automatic loser at double the bet.

The 10 factor is also an important strategic consideration, for it affects the dealer's busting potential. We double more aggressively against the weakest of the dealer stiff cards, the 4, 5 and

6, and less aggressively against the other stiff cards, the 2 and 3.

The only times we will double against the dealer pat cards are when our doubling totals of 10 and 11, hands that could turn into 20s and 21s, are powerful themselves.

Multiple Deck Doubling Strategy

You'll notice that the doubling strategies for multiple deck play are somewhat less aggressive than the single deck game, a difference we'll discuss later on.

In the following discussion, where multiple deck strategies differ from the single deck, an asterisk will denote the strategy change, and that change will be indicated.

Doubling 11*

This is the strongest doubling hand for the player and should be doubled against all the dealer upcards in a single deck game. If we draw a 10 value card on our double, we will have a 21, the strongest hand we can have. At best, the dealer can tie us.

*Do not double 11 vs. Ace in multiple deck games.

Doubling 10

This is the second strongest doubling hand and should be doubled against the dealer's 2-9. Our hard 10 gravitates toward a 20, an overwhelmingly strong hand against these upcards.

Doubling 9*

Double 9 against 2 through 6 only.* The high busting potential of the dealer stiff cards (2-6) makes the 9 a profitable double down. We cannot double down against any of the pat cards (7-Ace) for our win potential when we do draw the 10 (for a total of 19) is not strong enough to compensate for the times when we draw a poor card and cannot draw again.

*Do not double 9 vs. 2 in a multiple deck game.

Doubling 8

Doubling 8 vs. 5, 6 is a valid play in a single deck game only.* Our 8 gravitates toward an 18, only a fair total. However, the very high busting potential of the dealer 5 and 6 make this double a slight gain. Our 8 is not strong enough to make doubling against other dealer upcards a good play.

*Do not double 8 vs. any upcard in multiple deck.

Doubling Down - Soft Totals

The high concentration of 10s play a different role in soft doubling than in hard doubling, for instead of having a positive effect on our chances of making a good total, the drawing of 10 will not even give us a pat hand on many of these doubles.

Doubling with soft totals is generally a gain against weak dealer upcards. The 10 factor figures strongly in the dealer's chances of busting, while on the other hand, the drawing of small and medium cards will often improve our hand to competitive and winning totals.

Many beginners make the mistake of not capitalizing on these profitable hands. Make sure you do.

Doubling A2, A3, A4, A5[*]

Double A2, A3, A4, and A5 against the dealer's 4, 5, and 6.

The very high busting probabilities of the dealer's 4, 5 and 6 makes doubling with our A2 to A5 profitable for the player. Again, the drawing of a 10 value card does not help our total, but the high dealer busting factor gives us an edge.

We do not double against the 2 and 3, because the dealer will make just too many hands with these upcards. The same is more strikingly true with the dealer pat cards, 7 through Ace.

*Do not double A2 or A3 vs. 4 in a multiple deck game.

Doubling A6*

Double A6 vs. dealer 2, 3, 4, 5, and 6. The A6 is a more powerful double than the A2-A5, for the drawing of a 10 to the A6 will at least give us a pat total and a potential push against a dealer's 17. This "push" factor enables us to gain by doubling against the dealer's 2 and 3 despite the fact that the dealer will make more pat totals than with the weaker upcards 4, 5, and 6.

*Do not double A6 vs. 2 in a multiple deck game.

Doubling A7

Double A7 vs. 3, 4, 5, and 6. Our soft 18 is only a fair total and drawing an additional card won't risk the destruction of a powerful total such as a 19 or 20.

Soft 18 is a strong double against the weaker

dealer stiffs 4, 5, and 6, but differs from the soft 17 in that we do not double against the 2. A standing total of 18 vs. a 2 is a stronger winning hand and we do not want to risk the weakening of this hand by doubling and having to draw a card.

Doubling A8, A9

We have two very strong totals here and do not want to risk our excellent chances of winning by attempting to double.

Stand with these powerful hands - do not double.

SPLITTING PAIRS

Splitting can do two valuable things. It can turn one poor total into two stronger hands, such as splitting a hard 16 (8-8) into two hands of 8 each, and it effectively doubles our bet.

The decision to split requires a closer look for we must balance the standing total of our hand against the two proposed split hands, and see if the split and resultant doubling of our bet increases our expectation of winning.

Splitting Pairs - Multiple Deck

You'll notice that we'll split less aggressively against a multiple deck game than against a single deck one. On the other hand, when the game offers doubling after splitting, we get more aggressive.

What happens when a multiple deck game offers doubling after splitting? We'll cover each of the possibilities in turn, showing you the best way to play no matter the situation.

Splitting 99

We will examine the decision to split 99 first, for it is a good example of the thinking process involved in splitting. First of all, we should note that this hand totaling 18 is only "fair," not a powerful total like a 19 or 20.

Splitting 9s - Dealer shows a 2, 3, 4, 5, 6

Split 99 against these dealer stiff cards. Our 18 is a winner, but splitting the hand into two halves of 9 each is a big gain. Each starting hand of 9, because of the 10 factor, gravitates toward strong player totals of 19.

The high busting potential of the dealer stiff cards gives us an excellent opportunity to maximize our gain in an advantageous situation.

Splitting 9s - Dealer shows a 7

Stand with 99 vs. dealer 7. We figure the dealer for a 17. Our standing total of 18 is a stronger total and a big potential winner. While splitting 9s will also produce a positive expectation of winning, the risking of our fairly secure 18 against the 7 for two strong but chancy totals reduces the gain.

We have the dealer beat. Stand.

Splitting 9s - Dealer shows an 8

Splitting 99 against the dealer's 8 is a big gain.

Against the dealer's 8, we figure our 18 to be a potential push. However, by splitting the 18 into two separate hands of 9, we hope to turn our possible push into two potential winners. (Each 9 gravitates toward a total of 19, one point higher than the dealer's 18.)

Splitting 9s - Dealer shows a 9

Splitting 99 vs. the dealer's 9 is also a big gain.

Against the 9, our 18 is a losing total, but splitting the 18 into two totals of 9 each reduces our potential loss. Rather than one losing total of 18, we have two potential pushes.

Splitting 9s - Dealer shows a 10 or Ace

Do not split 99 against the dealer's 10 or Ace.

Our split hands of 9 gravitate toward good totals, but against these more powerful dealer upcards, splitting would be a poor play. We do not want to make one loser into two.

*Splitting 22 and 33**

Split 22 vs. dealer 3 through 7.*

Split 33 vs. dealer 4 through 7.*

The high busting probabilities of the dealer 4, 5 and 6 makes the 22 and 33 good splits. We split 22 vs. 3 and not 33 vs. 3, because of the lower player busting factor of our split hands of 2 each. The drawing of a 10 gives us another chance to improve on our 2, for correct basic strategy is to draw 12 vs. 3, while the drawing of a 10 on our 3 forces us to stand.

We do not split 22 or 33 vs. the dealer's 2, because the dealer's 2 does not bust often enough to make splitting a profitable play.

Splitting 22 and 33 vs. 7 seems unusual at first, for this play seems to exceed our normal strategic boundaries of making aggressive plays against the weak dealer stiff cards. Though the 7 is a pat card and will make a lot of pat hands, the 7 will also make the weakest totals, only gravitating toward a total of 17. Our starting totals of 2 and 3 will make hands of 18 or better about one-half the time.

Splitting 22 and 33 against the dealer's 7 will not make us money (because of the high busting factor of our hands), but they will produce a moderate gain over drawing to these hands.

Do not split 22 and 33 against the 8, 9, 10, or Ace. We do not want to make one loser into two losers.

*Multiple deck exception - Do not split 22 vs. 3.
**Games with doubling after splitting allowed (such as Atlantic City) - Split 22 and 33 vs. 2 through 7.

Splitting 44s**

Do not split 44 (unless doubling after splitting is allowed).

The hard total of 8 gravitates toward a total of 18, a far better position than two weak starting totals of 4 each. Against the dealer stiff cards, 2 through 6, we have a big gain by drawing to our 8. While the drawing of 10 will not give us an overwhelmingly strong total, an 18 is far better than drawing the same 10 to a split 4.

We do not want to hold two weak hands of 4 each against the dealer pat cards, especially the dealer's 7 and 8, where we have a good starting total of 8.

**Games with doubling after splitting allowed (such as Atlantic City) - Split 44 vs. 5 and 6. The added possibilities of being able to double our bet should either or both of the split totals pull well makes this split an advantageous move.

Splitting 55

Never split 55. 55 by itself is an excellent starting total of 10. You do not want to break up this powerful player total into two terrible hands of 5 each. (Our 10 is an excellent doubling hand against dealer upcards of 2 through 9.)

Splitting 66*

Split 66 against dealer stiff cards 2 through 6 only.* Our hard total of 12 is not very favorable, nor are the split hands of 6 and 6 too promising either. We have a losing hand either way against all dealer upcards. However, we want to minimize our losses.

Against the dealer stiff cards 2, 3, 4, 5, and 6, our split hands of 6 and 6 will sometimes draw cards to give us pat totals of 17-21.

Of course, we will often end up with stiff totals on the split pair (by the drawing of a 10 or other sufficiently large card) and be forced to stand. But the high dealer busting factor makes splitting 66 against the dealer stiffs a slight gain.

Obviously we will not split 66 against the dealer pat cards. We don't need two hands of 16 against a card that will bust only one time in four.

*Multiple deck exception - Do not split 66 vs. 2.
**Games with doubling after splitting allowed (such as Atlantic- City) - no exceptions. Split 66 vs. 2-6.

Splitting 77

Split 77 against dealer upcards of 2, 3, 4, 5, 6, and 7. Against the dealer stiff cards 2 through 6, two playable hands of 7 and 7 are preferable to one stiff total of 14. Splitting 77 is not a strong split, for these totals only gravitate toward a 17, but the high busting rate of the dealer stiff cards makes this split a big gain.

Splitting 77 against the dealer's 7 is also an excellent split, for we are taking one losing total of 14 into two potential pushes of 17 each.

We don't split 77 vs. the dealer's 8, 9, 10, and Ace. We do not want to take one poor total of 14 into two hands gravitating toward a second best total of only 17.

Splitting 88

Split 88 against all dealer upcards. Against the dealer's 2 through 8, we are taking one terrible hand of 16 into two playable totals of 8 each. There is a tremendous gain on all these plays.

Splitting 88 against the dealer's 9, 10, A are the strangest of the basic strategy plays. While splitting this 16 into two hands of 8 and 8 is not a winning situation against the strong dealer upcards of 9, 10, and A, it is an improvement over our very weak total of hard 16.

Bear with this unusual play, for computer simulation studies have played out the hand millions of times for both drawing and splitting, and found that the player loses less by splitting 88. Although this split is weak, it produces a gain over drawing to the easily bustable 16.

Splitting 10, 10

Do not split 10s. The hard total of 20 is a winning hand against all dealer upcards. Splitting 10s against any dealer upcard is a terrible play, for you are taking one "solid" winning hand into two good but uncertain wins.

Splitting AA

Split AA against all dealer upcards. Each Ace is a powerful starting total of 11 points. If we draw the 10, our 21 can't be beat. Splitting AA is a tremendous gain against all dealer upcards.

HOW TO USE THE STRATEGY CHARTS

In all our charts on the following pages, the dealer's upcard is indicated by the horizontal number (running left to right) on the top row, and the player's hand is indicted by the vertical numbers (up and down) in the left column. The letters in the matrix indicate the correct strategy play.

For example, in the following charts, if you're dealt an A6 and the dealer shows a 7 as an upcard, the "H" in the matrix shows that hitting is the correct play.

Strategy when Doubling Down is Restricted

In Northern Nevada and other locations where doubling is restricted, usually to 10 and 11, hit instead of doubling on all hands where "D" is indicated, except on A7, where you should stand.

Atlantic City, European Master Charts

The Atlantic City Charts reflect more aggressive doubling than the Las Vegas multiple deck charts due to doubling after splitting, while the European chart shows less frequent doubling and splitting due to the restricted doubling on 9-11 only and the No Hole Card Rule (see page 73).

SINGLE DECK MASTER CHART

	2	3	4	5	6	7	8	9	10	A
7/less	H	H	H	H	H	H	H	H	H	H
62	H	H	H	H	H	H	H	H	H	H
44/53	H	H	H	D	D	H	H	H	H	H
9	D	D	D	D	D	H	H	H	H	H
10	D	D	D	D	D	D	D	D	H	H
11	D	D	D	D	D	D	D	D	D	D
12	H	H	S	S	S	H	H	H	H	H
13	S	S	S	S	S	H	H	H	H	H
14	S	S	S	S	S	H	H	H	H	H
15	S	S	S	S	S	H	H	H	H	H
16	S	S	S	S	S	H	H	H	H	H
A2	H	H	D	D	D	H	H	H	H	H
A3	H	H	D	D	D	H	H	H	H	H
A4	H	H	D	D	D	H	H	H	H	H
A5	H	H	D	D	D	H	H	H	H	H
A6	D	D	D	D	D	H	H	H	H	H
A7	S	D	D	D	D	S	S	H	H	H
A8	S	S	S	S	S	S	S	S	S	S
A9	S	S	S	S	S	S	S	S	S	S
22	H	spl	spl	spl	spl	spl	H	H	H	H
33	H	H	spl	spl	spl	spl	H	H	H	H
44	H	H	H	D	D	H	H	H	H	H
55	D	D	D	D	D	D	D	D	H	H
66	spl	spl	spl	spl	spl	H	H	H	H	H
77	spl	spl	spl	spl	spl	spl	H	H	H	H
88	spl	spl	spl	spl	spl	spl	spl	spl	spl	spl
99	spl	spl	spl	spl	spl	S	spl	spl	S	S
10/10	S	S	S	S	S	S	S	S	S	S
AA	spl	spl	spl	spl	spl	spl	spl	spl	spl	spl

S = Stand   H = Hit   D = Double   spl = Split

MULTIPLE DECK MASTER CHART

	2	3	4	5	6	7	8	9	10	A
7/less	H	H	H	H	H	H	H	H	H	H
62	H	H	H	H	H	H	H	H	H	H
44/53	H	H	H	H	H	H	H	H	H	H
9	H	D	D	D	D	H	H	H	H	H
10	D	D	D	D	D	D	D	D	H	H
11	D	D	D	D	D	D	D	D	D	H
12	H	H	S	S	S	H	H	H	H	H
13	S	S	S	S	S	H	H	H	H	H
14	S	S	S	S	S	H	H	H	H	H
15	S	S	S	S	S	H	H	H	H	H
16	S	S	S	S	S	H	H	H	H	H
A2	H	H	H	D	D	H	H	H	H	H
A3	H	H	H	D	D	H	H	H	H	H
A4	H	H	D	D	D	H	H	H	H	H
A5	H	H	D	D	D	H	H	H	H	H
A6	H	D	D	D	D	H	H	H	H	H
A7	S	D	D	D	D	S	S	H	H	H
A8	S	S	S	S	S	S	S	S	S	S
A9	S	S	S	S	S	S	S	S	S	S
22	H	H	spl	spl	spl	spl	H	H	H	H
33	H	H	spl	spl	spl	spl	H	H	H	H
44	H	H	H	H	H	H	H	H	H	H
55	D	D	D	D	D	D	D	D	H	H
66	H	spl	spl	spl	spl	H	H	H	H	H
77	spl	spl	spl	spl	spl	spl	H	H	H	H
88	spl	spl	spl	spl	spl	spl	spl	spl	spl	spl
99	spl	spl	spl	spl	spl	S	spl	spl	S	S
10/10	S	S	S	S	S	S	S	S	S	S
AA	spl	spl	spl	spl	spl	spl	spl	spl	spl	spl

S = Stand   H = Hit   D = Double   spl = Split

ATLANTIC CITY MULTIPLE DECK MASTER CHART

	2	3	4	5	6	7	8	9	10	A
7/less	H	H	H	H	H	H	H	H	H	H
62	H	H	H	H	H	H	H	H	H	H
44/53	H	H	H	H	H	H	H	H	H	H
9	H	D	D	D	D	H	H	H	H	H
10	D	D	D	D	D	D	D	D	H	H
11	D	D	D	D	D	D	D	D	D	H
12	H	H	S	S	S	H	H	H	H	H
13	S	S	S	S	S	H	H	H	H	H
14	S	S	S	S	S	H	H	H	H	H
15	S	S	S	S	S	H	H	H	H	H
16	S	S	S	S	S	H	H	H	H	H
A2	H	H	H	D	D	H	H	H	H	H
A3	H	H	H	D	D	H	H	H	H	H
A4	H	H	D	D	D	H	H	H	H	H
A5	H	H	D	D	D	H	H	H	H	H
A6	H	D	D	D	D	H	H	H	H	H
A7	S	D	D	D	D	S	S	H	H	H
A8	S	S	S	S	S	S	S	S	S	S
A9	S	S	S	S	S	S	S	S	S	S
22	spl	spl	spl	spl	spl	spl	H	H	H	H
33	spl	spl	spl	spl	spl	spl	H	H	H	H
44	H	H	H	spl	spl	H	H	H	H	H
55	D	D	D	D	D	D	D	D	H	H
66	H	spl	spl	spl	spl	H	H	H	H	H
77	spl	spl	spl	spl	spl	spl	H	H	H	H
88	spl	spl	spl	spl	spl	spl	spl	spl	spl	spl
99	spl	spl	spl	spl	spl	S	spl	spl	S	S
10/10	S	S	S	S	S	S	S	S	S	S
AA	spl	spl	spl	spl	spl	spl	spl	spl	spl	spl

S = Stand   H = Hit   D = Double   spl = Split

EUROPEAN-STYLE MULTIPLE DECK MASTER CHART

	2	3	4	5	6	7	8	9	10	A
7/less	H	H	H	H	H	H	H	H	H	H
62	H	H	H	H	H	H	H	H	H	H
44/53	H	H	H	H	H	H	H	H	H	H
9	H	D	D	D	D	H	H	H	H	H
10	D	D	D	D	D	D	D	D	H	H
11	D	D	D	D	D	D	D	D	H	H
12	H	H	S	S	S	H	H	H	H	H
13	S	S	S	S	S	H	H	H	H	H
14	S	S	S	S	S	H	H	H	H	H
15	S	S	S	S	S	H	H	H	H	H
16	S	S	S	S	S	H	H	H	H	H
A2	H	H	H	H	H	H	H	H	H	H
A3	H	H	H	H	H	H	H	H	H	H
A4	H	H	H	H	H	H	H	H	H	H
A5	H	H	H	H	H	H	H	H	H	H
A6	H	H	H	H	H	H	H	H	H	H
A7	S	S	S	S	S	S	S	H	H	H
A8	S	S	S	S	S	S	S	S	S	S
A9	S	S	S	S	S	S	S	S	S	S
22	H	H	spl	spl	spl	spl	H	H	H	H
33	H	H	spl	spl	spl	spl	H	H	H	H
44	H	H	H	H	H	H	H	H	H	H
55	D	D	D	D	D	D	D	D	H	H
66	H	spl	spl	spl	spl	H	H	H	H	H
77	spl	spl	spl	spl	spl	spl	H	H	H	H
88	spl	spl	spl	spl	spl	spl	spl	spl	spl	spl
99	spl	spl	spl	spl	spl	S	spl	spl	S	S
10/10	S	S	S	S	S	S	S	S	S	S
AA	spl	spl	spl	spl	spl	spl	spl	spl	spl	spl

S = Stand   H = Hit   D = Double   spl = Split

SINGLE & MULTIPLE DECK DIFFERENCES

The greater number of cards used in a multiple deck game makes the removal of any particular card or cards less significant compared to a single deck game, and as a result, our doubling and splitting strategies are less aggressive.

For example, the removal of three cards (5,3,5) creates a favorable imbalance for the player in a single deck game and makes a 53 double vs. the dealer's 5 a profitable play. The effective removal of these cards gives the player a better chance of drawing a 10 on his 8 and, at the same time, increases the dealer's chance of busting.

However, the removal of these three cards are barely felt in a multiple deck game, and thus, no favorable imbalance has been created and the double down is not a correct play. This lack of sensitivity to particular card removal in multiple deck games accounts for the following nine changes in the doubling and splitting strategies.

Otherwise, multiple deck basic strategy is identical to the single deck basic strategy.

IN A MULTIPLE DECK GAME

- Do not double hard 8 vs. 5; hit instead.
- Do not double hard 8 vs. 6; hit instead.
- Do not double hard 9 vs. 2; hit instead.
- Do not double hard 11 vs. Ace; hit instead.
- Do not double A2 vs 4; hit instead.
- Do not double A3 vs. 4; hit instead.
- Do not double A6 vs 2; hit instead.
- Do not split 22 vs. 3; hit instead.
- Do not split 66 vs. 2; hit instead.

European No Hole Card Rule

The predominant style of play in casinos outside the United States is for the dealer to take his second card after all the players have acted upon their hands. The disadvantage to the player is that on hands doubled or split, the additional moneys bet will be lost if indeed the dealer has a blackjack. As you'll see, in the European No Hole Card Rules chart, we'll adjust our strategies accordingly when playing in these games, being less aggressive in doubling and splitting situations, so as to minimize the negative effect of this rule.

PLAYER'S OPTIONS

Use these strategies where permitted:

Doubling Down Permitted After Splitting

A standard option in Atlantic City, but offered only in a few Nevada casinos. It allows you to double down on one or more of the hands resulting from a split according to the standard doubling rules of the casino.

When this option is permitted, you'll split more aggressively to take advantage of good doubling situations that can arise as a consequence of the split.

This option is favorable to the player.

Our Hand		Single Deck	Multiple Deck
22	split against	2-7	2-7
33	split against	2-7	2-7
44	split against	4-6	5-6
66	split against	2-7	2-6
77	split against	2-8	2-7

WINNING AT BLACKJACK

Late Surrender (Surrender)

A player option to forfeit his hand and lose half his bet after it has been determined that the dealer does not have a blackjack. This option is favorable to the player.

Our Hand		Single Deck	Multiple Deck
16*	surrender against	10, A	9, 10, A
15	surrender against	10	10
77	surrender against	10	-

*Split 88 - Do not surrender

Early Surrender

A player option to forfeit his hand and lose half his bet *before* the dealer checks for a black-jack. A rare option, but extremely valuable for the player if available.

Dealer's Upcard	Player's Totals
A early surrender with	5-7, 12-17
10 early surrender with	14-16
9 early surrender with	16*

Do not surrender soft totals
*Split 88 - Do not early surrender

WINNING STRATEGIES

By following the basics strategies we showed earlier, you're already starting with an even or near even game.* These playing strategies make you better than 95% of the players who play the game. In money terms, that gives you a dead even game under certain conditions, or near break-even in others. Already, that is a huge improvement!

To get an actual mathematical advantage over the casino and the expectation to win money every time you play, requires the use of professional card counting or non-counting techniques.

While professional strategies are beyond the scope of this work, (see ads in the back for more information) we'll show you a few basic principles to increase the strength of your game.

First, we must understand the nature of blackjack and we'll begin with the cards themselves and how they relate to your chances of winning.

*If you play perfect basic strategy as we've shown, and the game is a single deck game with the favorable Las Vegas Strip rules, the game is dead-even - the house has no edge on you! If the particular game has less liberal rules (Northern Nevada) or is a multiple deck game, the house enjoys a slight initial edge.

WINNING AT BLACKJACK

The Value of the Cards

Tens and Aces are the most valuable cards for the player. When there is a higher ratio of these cards in the deck than normal, the odds shift in the player's favor. Conversely, when there is a smaller ratio of these high cards in the deck, meaning there are more smaller cards (2 through 7) than normal, cards that favor the house, the odds shift in the casino's favor. The 8s and 9s are relatively neutral.

You can achieve an extra edge in blackjack by playing an "eyeballing strategy." When a lot of tens and aces seem to have been already played, more than the normal amount, you bet less. The aces and tens are cards you need in the deck. On the other hand, when a lot of small cards (more than normal) have been played, than you bet more. The valuable tens and Aces remain in abundance and thus you are in a favorable situation.

Every time the deck is shuffled, start your estimation of tens and aces over again. We're tracking cards dealt from a depleted deck of cards. Once the deck has been shuffled, the game is fresh and we must begin fresh.

This simple strategy is most effective in single

deck blackjack, and less so, incrementally, in two, four, six and eight deck games where the overall number of the cards is less susceptible to composition changes from just a few cards being removed.

Obviously, you cannot win as much without using professional card counting or non-counting techniques, but combining the eyeballing strategy with the basic strategies we've presented gives you a very strong game against any casino.

Bet Range

I recommend a single deck bet range of 1-4 units. Thus, if $5 is your standard bet, your maximum bet should be $20. Similarly, $10 bettors should hold their maximum bet to $40, $25 bettors to $100, and $100 bettors to $400.

The ranging of your bets from one unit in disadvantageous situations to four units in highly advantageous situations is a wide enough bet spread to maximize your gains while at the same time minimizing your risk.

Multiple deck players need a wider bet spread than 1-4 to be effective, but this only make sense if you're armed with a professional strategy.

WINNING AT BLACKJACK

Making Money at Blackjack

If you want to be a consistent winner at black-jack and have a mathematical edge, the first thing you must do is learn the optimal basic strategies in this book. All advanced strategies assume this knowledge. This is true in single and multiple deck games. Then you must learn a professional non-counting or counting strategy to get the edge.

The best strategy to pursue if you're a casual player that wants to take his or her game to the next level is to get the easy-to-use Cardoza 1-2-3 Multiple Deck Non-Counter Strategy. This will give you a mathematical edge of about 1/2-1%. This strategy was developed for players who want to beat the multiple deck game but are intimi-dated by card counting. The 1-2-3 Non-Counter is only available through Cardoza Publishing.

The second choice is the Cardoza Base Count Strategy, or even better, the home instruction course, (which includes the Base Count Strategy) designed for serious players who want to work just a little harder.

These card counting strategies give you an edge of from 1-3% over the casino and put you on a professional level of play. You'll learn advanced betting and playing strategies and receive full strategy charts that will prepare you for every situation. No longer will those 15s and 16s be busted with big bets on the table!

These card counting strategies and the exciting new Multiple Deck Non-Counter can be ordered through the coupons in the back of the book.

Winning Summary

We've covered a lot of ground in this section, showing you how to play your hands and how to optimally use all the options available at blackjack. A lot of money can be made at blackjack, which is why the game is so popular, but as you see, you must invest a little time in learning how to play the game properly.

Blackjack is a percentage game that can be beat, but to win, you've got to stick by your guns, and always make the correct percentage plays as we've showed you here. Thse strategies are computer-proven and 100% accurate. You won't win every hand, nor will you win every session. However, with correct play, you can be an overall winner at blackjack.

Good Skill!

WINNING AT CRAPS

INTRODUCTION

Craps is the most exciting of the casino games, for the action is fast, and a player catching a good roll can win large sums of money quickly. But big money can be lost just as fast unless the player is conversant with the best bets available and knows how to use them in a coordinated strategy.

We'll go over the fundamentals of playing casino craps in this section, and not only explain all the bets available and show you which wagers are the best to make, but also, we'll show you how to play these bets so that when the smoke clears, you'll have the best chances of emerging a winner.

Let's get on with it, and let the dice roll!

BEGINNER'S GUIDE TO CASINO CRAPS

The Table

The standard casino craps table is oval in shape and depending upon the particular size is built to accommodate between 15 to 24 players.

The sides of the table are several feet above the layout where the bets are made, giving the players an edge to lean on, and giving the dice walls to carom off.

The Layout

The craps layout is divided into three distinct sections. The two end sections, which are identical, are areas around which the players cluster, and where the majority of bets are made. Each end area is run by one of the standing dealers.

The middle area is flanked on either side by a boxman and stickman. This area contains the proposition, or center bets, and is completely under the jurisdiction of the stickman.

The layout is a large piece of green felt with various imprints marking the plethora of bets possible. All action is centered on the layout. Bets are placed, paid off and collected on this felt surface. And, of course, it is on the layout where the dice are thrown.

Layouts around the world are basically the same, though some clubs may have slight variations, but none of these need concern us, for the game of craps is similar whatever casino you play in. The minor variations that do occur, concern bets whose odds are so poor that we wouldn't want to make them anyway.

The following page shows a standard craps layout.

The Dice

The game of craps is played with two standard six-sided dice, with each die numbered from 1 to 6. The dice are manufactured so that they fall as randomly as possible, with a 5 being just as likely to fall on one die as a 3. However, we'll see later that combining two dice together creates some combinations that are more likely to appear than others, and this is the basis of the odds in craps.

The Craps Layout

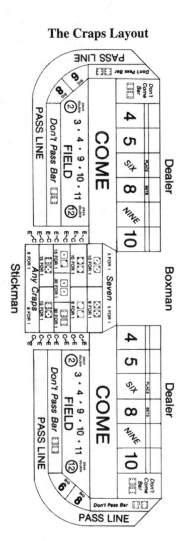

WINNING AT CRAPS

Players

Only one player is needed to play craps, while as many as can fit around a craps table are the maximum. When the action is hot and heavy, bettors will be lined up shoulder to shoulder, screaming, yelling and cajoling, for the dice to come through and make them winners.

Casino Personnel

The average craps table is manned by a crew of four casino employees - one **stickman**, who stands at the center of the table, two **dealers**, who stand on the opposite side of the stickman at either end of the table, and a **boxman** who is seated between the two standing dealers and directly across from the stickman.

Let's look at the function of each crewman in turn.

The Stickman

The **stickman's** main responsibility is the handling of the dice, a task he performs with a flexible, hooked stick. When a new shooter is coming-out, the stickman will offer him a cache of dice to choose from, and after two have been selected, will return the remaining dice to his box.

After each roll of the dice, the stickman will announce the number thrown and bring the dice back to the center of the table. Usually, he will supply additional information about its consequences.

If a 7 is thrown on the come-out roll, he may announce, "7, winner on the pass line."

If instead, a 2, 3 or 12 is rolled on the come-out, he may say, "Craps, line away." When a shooter sevens-out, the stickman might exclaim, "7 out, line away."

A good stickman is a show in himself, and by the excitement he generates, makes the game more lively and colorful for both the players and the dealers. And from the casino's standpoint, happy players tend to bet heavier and wilder than they normally would.

The dice will be returned to the shooter after the dealers have finished making payoffs.

The stickman is also responsible for the proposition, or center bets made in the middle of the layout. He will place all proposition bets directed his way into their proper location on the layout.

If these bets are winners, the stickman will direct the dealers to pay off the winning players, and if the bets are losers, he will collect the lost bets and push them over to the boxman.

The Dealers

There is a dealer located on either side of the boxman, and his main responsibility is the handling of all the monetary transactions and betting on his end of the table. He pays off winning bets and collects losing ones, converts cash into chips, and will change chips into higher or lower denominations for the player.

Though the player can make many of the bets himself, there are wagers such as the place bets and certain free-odds bets which must be given to the dealer to be placed.

Each standing dealer has a **marker buck**, a plastic disk used to indicate the established point. If a player is coming-out, beginning his roll, the marker buck will be lying on its black side, labeled "**off**," and if a point is established, the dealer will flip the marker buck to the white side, marked "**on**," and place it in the appropriately numbered box to indicate the point.

It is with the dealers that the player will have most of his contact and to whom he can address his questions.

The Boxman

The **boxman** sits between the two dealers and across from the stickman, and from this central position, supervises the running of the craps table. His job is not only to watch over the casinos bankroll, most of which sits right in front of him in huge stacks, but to make sure the dealers make the correct payoffs so that neither the player nor the house gets shorted.

He is responsible for settling any disputes that may arise between the players and the dealers. Generally, the benefit of the doubt will be given to the player on any disputed call. If the dice leave the table for any reason, the returned dice are brought directly to the boxman for inspection. He'll check the logo and coded numbers on the dice to make sure they haven't been switched, and will inspect the surfaces for imperfections that may influence the game. If, for any reason, the boxman feels suspicious of the returned dice, he'll remove them from play and have the stickman offer the shooter a new pair.

When one boxman is on duty, he will supervise one end of the table while the stickman watches the other.

However, when the action is fast, and stacks of chips are riding on each roll of the dice, a second boxman will often be added to the crew to help watch the table. In these cases, the boxmen will sit next to each other behind the chips, each being responsible for one end of the table.

In addition to the boxmen, there are other supervisors, called floormen and pit bosses, who watch over the action from behind the boxman in the area known as the pit.

The Pit

Craps tables are arranged in a pattern so that a central area, known as the **pit**, is formed in the middle. The tables are arranged around the pit so that the boxmen and standing dealers have their backs to the pit area, and so that the floormen, standing inside the pit, can easily watch over all of the craps tables.

Floormen

The **floormen** spend their entire shift on their feet, and are responsible for supervising a particular table or group of tables in the pit.

In addition to these supervisory capacities, they deal with players that have established credit lines. If a player requests credit, the floorman checks to see if his credit is good, and if verified, authorizes the dealer to give the requested chips. At the same time, or soon afterwards, he will bring the player an IOU to sign, acknowledging the credit transaction.

The Pit Boss

The **pit boss**, under whose authority the floormen work, is in charge of the entire craps pit. He's rarely in contact with the players, unless a high roller is playing, whereby he may come over and introduce himself or offer the roller some **comps** (freebies).

Entering a Game

To enter a craps game, slip into a space by the rail of the craps table. After catching the dealer's attention, place your cash on the layout and inform him of the denomination of chips you would like. The dealer will take your money, and give it to the boxman who will supervise the exchange.

Tipping

Tips are shared by the crew working the craps table. Though the usual tip is to make a proposition bet, with the exclamation "one for the boys," a better way to toke the crew would be to make a line bet for them, so they can have a good chance of winning the bet.

Dealers prefer this type of tip for they too are aware how poor the proposition bets are. This is also better than just handing over the toke, for if the bet is won, the dealer wins double for the tip - the amount bet for him plus the winnings from that bet.

Play of the Game

When a new player is to throw the dice, the stickman will empty his box of dice and push them across the layout with his stick. After this player, known as the **shooter**, selects two dice of his choice, the stickman will retrieve the remaining dice and return them to his box.

In a new game, the player closest to the boxman's left side will receive the dice first, and the rotation of the dice will go clockwise from player to player around the craps table.

The shooter has no advantage over the other players except perhaps the psychological edge he may get throwing the dice himself. He is required to make either a pass or don't pass bet as the shooter, and in addition, can make any other bets allowed.

There are a wide variety of bets the players can make, and these bets should be placed before the shooter throws the dice. Players can bet with the dice or against them at their preference, but in either case, the casino will book all wagers.

The shooter is supposed to throw the dice so that they bounce off the far wall of the table. If the throw does not reach the far wall, the shooter will be requested to toss harder on his next throw, and if he persists in underthrowing the dice, the boxman may disallow him from throwing further.

This policy protects against cheats that can manipulate unobstructed throws of the dice.

The Come-Out Roll

The first throw of a shoot is called the **come-out roll**. It is either an automatic winner or loser for players betting with the dice, called **right bettors**, or those betting against the dice, called

wrong bettors; or the come-out roll can establish a point which the shooter hopes to repeat before a 7 is thrown.

The come-out roll works as follows. The throw of a 7 or 11 on the come-out roll is an automatic winner for the pass line bettors, players betting that the dice will win, or pass, while the throw of a **craps**, a 2, 3 or 12 is an automatic loser.

For the don't pass bettors, those betting against the dice, the come-out roll works almost exactly opposite to the pass line bet. A come-out roll of a 7 or an 11 is an automatic loser, a 2 or a 3 an automatic winner, while the 12 (in some casinos a 2 instead) is a standoff.

If the come-out roll is an automatic decision, a 2, 3, 7, 11 or 12, the affected players will have their bets paid or collected, and the following roll will be a new come-out roll.

Any other number thrown, a 4, 5, 6, 8, 9 or 10, becomes the **point**, and the dealers will indicate this by flipping their respective marker bucks to the white side marked "on," and move the disk into the rectangular numbered boxes corresponding to the point number thrown.

Once a point is established, only the 7 and the point are consequential rolls for the pass and don't pass bettors, also called **line bettors**. All other rolls are neutral throws for these bets.

The shoot will continue until either the point is repeated, a winner for the pass line bettors and a loser for the don't pass bettors, or until a seven is thrown, known as **sevening-out**, a loser on the pass line and winner on the don't pass. In either case, the shoot will have been completed, and the following roll will be a new come-out roll, the start of a new shoot.

There are many other bets available to the player as we will discuss later, some that can be made only after a point is established, and others that can be made at any time during a shoot. So while the line bettors may not be affected by a particular throw, the dealers may be paying off or collecting chips on other affected wagers while the shoot is in progress.

The shooter can continue throwing the dice until he sevens-out. Then, after all affected bets are settled on the layout, the stickman will present his collection of dice to the next player in a clockwise rotation. Even though the shooter may **crap-out** (the throw of a 2, 3 or 12) on his come-out roll, a losing roll for the pass line bettors, the shooter does not have to yield the dice.

It is only when the shooter throws a 7 before his point repeats, *sevens-out*, that the dice must be relinquished.

The Come-Out Roll Capsulated
The come-out roll occurs when:
• A new shooter takes the dice.
• The shooter throws a 2, 3, 7, 11 or 12 on the come-out roll, an automatic winner or loser for the line bettors.
• After a point is established, the shooter either repeats that point or sevens-out.

Betting Right or Wrong
Betting right or wrong are only casino terms used to designate whether a player is betting with the dice, **betting right**, or betting against the dice, **betting wrong**, and are in no way indicative of a correct or incorrect way of playing. As we shall see, both ways of betting are equally valid.

UNDERSTANDING THE ODDS
Craps is played with two dice, individually called die, and each die is a near perfect six-

sided cube, guaranteed to be within 1/10,000 of an inch accurate.

Each die has six equally possible outcomes when thrown - numbers one through six. The two dice thrown together have a total of 36 possible outcomes, the six combinations of one die by the six combinations of the other.

The chart below shows these combinations.

COMBINATIONS OF THE DICE

Result	Odds of Result
2	1 out of 36
3	2 out of 36
4	3 out of 36
5	4 out of 36
6	5 out of 36
7	6 out of 36
8	5 out of 36
9	4 out of 36
10	3 out of 36
11	2 out of 36
12	1 out of 36
Total	**36 out of 36**

WINNING AT CRAPS

You can see by the chart that the 7 is more likely to be thrown than any other number, having six possible combinations.

Next in frequency are the 6 and the 8, five outcomes each, then the 5 and the 9, four outcomes, the 4 and the 10, three outcomes apiece, the 3 and the 11, two outcomes, and finally, the 2 and the 12, one combination each.

A Shortcut to Remembering the Odds

Notice the symmetry of combinations on either side of the 7. The 6 and 8 have equal possibilities of being thrown, just as the 5 and 9, 4 and 10, 3 and 11, and 2 and 12 do.

If you take rolls of 7 and below and subtract one from that number, you arrive at the correct number of combinations for that roll. Thus, there are four ways to roll a 5 (5-1), six ways to roll a 7 (7-1) and one way to roll a 2 (2-1).

For numbers greater than the 7, match that number with the corresponding symmetrical number on the other side of the 7, and subtract one. Thus, to find the combinations of the 8, you match it with the 6 (which has an equal likelihood of occurring), and subtracting one, you get five combinations.

Figuring the Odds of Rolling a Specific Number

To figure the odds of rolling any particular number, divide the number of combinations for that particular number into 36, the total number of combinations possible.

Let's say the 7. There are six ways to roll a 7. Dividing the six combinations into 36, the total number of combinations, we find the odds of rolling a 7 on any one roll is one in six (6/36 reduced to 1/6), or equivalently, 5 to 1. The chart following shows the odds of rolling a number on any one roll.

ODDS OF ROLLING THE NUMBERS

The Roll	Combinations	Chance of Being Rolled	Odds Against
2 or 12	1	1/36	35 to 1
3 or 11	2	2/36	17 to 1
4 or 10	3	3/36	11 to 1
5 or 9	4	4/36	8 to 1
6 or 8	5	5/36	6 .2 to 1
7	6	6/36	5 to 1

Understanding The Terminology-Correct Odds, House Payoff & Edge

The house advantage or edge is the difference between the player's chances of winning the bet, called the **correct odds**, and the casino's actual payoff, called the **house payoff** or simply, the **payoff**. For example, the correct odds of rolling a 7 are 5 to 1. Since the house will pay only 4 to 1 should the 7 be thrown, they maintain an edge of 16.67 percent on this wager.

To play craps intelligently and better understand the choices available to him, the player must first and foremost be aware of the house advantage on every bet he will ever make, for that, in the long run, determines the player's chances of winning.

Five for One, Five to One

Sometimes on a layout you will see payoffs represented as *for* instead of the usual *to*, such as 9 for 1. This means that the payoff will be a total of nine units, eight winning chips along with your original bet, a house subterfuge to increase its edge over the player. The usual 9 to 1 payoff means nine winning chips and your original bet returned, for a total of 10 units.

Beware of any payoffs with the *for*. As a rule, this type of bet has poor odds to begin with and we wouldn't want to make it anyway, with the *to* or the *for*.

The Bets

Craps offers the player a wide variety of possible wagers, with each bet having its own characteristics and inherent odds. Some bets, which we will refer to as **sequence bets**, may require a series of rolls before the outcome is determined, while the outcome of others, called **one-roll bets**, is determined on the very next roll.

Some bets are paid off by the house at **even-money**, for every dollar wagered, the player wins a dollar, while other bets have payoffs as high as 30 to 1. However, as you will see, generally the higher the house payoff, the worse the odds are.

And the odds of the bet, that is, the mathematical house return on every dollar wagered, is the most important concern of the player. To have the best chances of winning, you must avoid all the sucker bets, and make only the best bets available.

THE BEST BETS

The bets presented in this section have the lowest built-in house edge of all the bets in craps, and one bet, the free-odds bet, gives the house no advantage whatsoever. These bets, the pass, don't pass, come, don't come and the free-odds bets, are the most important bets a player can make, and are the foundation of our winning strategies.

The Line Bets: Pass & Don't Pass

These even-money bets can only be made on a come-out roll, before a point is established, and give the house an edge of only 1.4 percent. And when backed by the free-odds wagers, the overall house edge drops to 0.8 percent in a single odds game and to 0.6 percent in a double odds game.

Pass Line

Players making pass line bets are wagering that the dice will **pass**, or win, and are called right bettors. Pass line bets are also referred to as **front line bets**, and are made by placing the wager in the area marked *pass line*.

On the come-out roll, a throw of a 7 or 11 is an automatic winner for the pass line bettors while the throw of a craps, a 2, 3 or 12 is an automatic loser. If any other number is thrown, the 4, 5, 6, 8, 9 or 10, then that number is established as the **point**, and the shooter must repeat the point before a 7 is thrown for pass line bettors to win. The throw of a 7 before the point repeats is a loser for pass line bettors, called **sevening-out**, and the dealers will collect the lost bets.

Once the point is established, only the 7 and the point number affect the pass line bettor. All other numbers have no bearing on the bet and can be considered neutral throws.

Let's look at three progressions to see how the pass line bet works.

1. The come-out roll is a 5, establishing 5 as the point. The following roll is a 2, a neutral throw, for a point has already been established. An 8 is then thrown, also neutral, and then a 5. The point was repeated, or made, before the seven was thrown, and the pass line bettors win their bets.

2. The come-out roll is a 7, an automatic winner for the pass line bettors. Since the progression is completed, the following roll will be another come-out roll.

3. Here's a losing proposition. The come-out roll is a 9, establishing 9 as the point. The shooter then rolls a 6, 12, and 11, all neutral rolls since a point is already established. Then a 7 is thrown. Since the 7 was rolled before the 9, the shooter's point repeated, pass line bettors lose and the dealer will collect their bets. A new come-out roll will ensue.

Pass Line Capsulated

> **Payoff**: Even -Money   **House Edge**: 1.4%
> **Automatic Winners** - 7 or 11 on the come-out roll.
> **Automatic Losers** - 2, 3, or 12 on the come-out roll.
>
> ---
>
> *Once a point is established, the pass line bettor:*
> **Wins** by the point repeating before the 7 is thrown.
> **Loses** by the roll of a 7 before the point repeats.

Don't Pass

Players betting don't pass are called wrong bettors, and are betting against the dice. Don't pass bets are also called **back line bets** and are made by placing the wager in the area marked *don't pass*.

On the come-out roll, a throw of a 2 or 3 is an automatic winner for the don't pass bettors, while a 7 or an 11 is an automatic loser. The 12 is a standoff between the back line bettor and the house. (In some casinos the 2 is the standoff and the 12 is the automatic winner. Either way it makes no difference, for there is only one way to throw the 2 or 12.)

Once the point is established, don't pass bettors win by having the 7 thrown before the shooter repeats his point, and lose by the point being repeated before the shooter sevens-out. Here are some progressions to illustrate the don't pass wager.

• The come-out roll is a 6, establishing 6 as the point. The following rolls are a 5 (no bearing on the outcome), then a 12 (still no bearing) and then a 7. Since the 7 was rolled before the 6 repeated, don't pass bettors win.

• The come-out roll is a 3, an automatic winner for the don't pass bettor.

• The come-out roll is a 4, establishing 4 as the point. A 3 is then rolled (neutral), and then a 4, a loss for the back line bettors since the point repeated before the 7 was rolled.

Don't Pass Line Capsulated

> **Payoff**: Even-Money   **House Edge**: 1.4%
> **Automatic Winners** - 2 (or 12) and 3 on the come-out roll.
> **Automatic Losers** - 7 or 11 on the come-out roll.
> **Standoff** - 12 (or 2 in some casinos) on the come-out roll.
>
> ———————————————————
>
> *Once a point is established, don't pass bettors:*
> **Win** by the throw of a 7 before the point repeats.
> **Lose** by the point repeating before the 7 thrown.

Come and Don't Come Bets

The come and don't come bets work according to the same rules as the pass and don't pass bets except that the come and don't come bets can only be made *after* a point is established. The line bets, on the other hand, can only be placed on a come-out roll, before a point is established.

The advantage of these bets are that they allow the player to cover more points as a right or wrong bettor at the same low 1.4% house edge. And like the line bets, the overall house edge drops to 0.8% when backed by single odds, and

0.6% when backed by double odds.

Come bets are made by putting the chips into the area marked *come*, while don't come bets are placed in the *don't come box*. Won bets are paid at even-money.

Come Bets

We follow the play of the come bets just as we would with the pass line bets. A 7 or 11 on the first throw following the placing of the bet is an automatic winner, while a 2, 3 or 12 is an automatic loser.

Any other number thrown, the 4, 5, 6, 8, 9 or 10, becomes the point for that come bet, called the **come point**, and the dealer will move the bet from the come box into the large rectangular numbered boxes located at the top of the layout to mark the come point.

Once the come point is established, the bet is won if the come point repeats before the shooter sevens-out, and lost if the 7 is rolled before the point repeats. All other throws are inconsequential on this bet. Won bets will be paid off and removed from the layout.

The bettor can make continuous come bets until all the points are covered if he desires. Thus, it is possible for the throw of a 7 to simultaneously wipe out several established come bets. On the other hand, a hot shooter rolling point numbers can bring frequent winners to the aggressive come bettor.

Let's follow a progression where the right bettor makes both pass line and come bets.

Player Bets $5 on the pass line. *The come-out roll is a 5*, establishing 5 as the point.

Player Bets $5 on the come. *The roll is an 8*, establishing 8 as the come point. The dealer moves the $5 come bet to the rectangular box marked 8 to indicate that 8 is the point for that come bet. In effect, the player has two points working, the 5 and the 8, and decides to make another come bet.

Player Bets $5 on the come. *The roll is a 6*. The dealer moves this new bet to the 6, the come point for this bet. The other two points are not affected by this roll. The player has three points established, the 5, 6 and 8, and makes no more bets at this time.

The roll is a 5, a $5 winner on the pass line. It is paid off and removed from the layout, leaving the player with two come points, the 6 and 8.

Player Bets $5 on the pass line. Since the next roll is a come-out roll and the player wants to cover another point, he bets the pass. ***The roll is a 10***, establishing 10 as the point.

Player makes no additional bets at this time. ***The roll is a 2*** (neutral on all established bets), then ***an 8 is thrown***, a $5 winner on the come point of 8, and that bet is paid off and removed.

The following roll is not a come-out roll, for the come point was made, not the pass line point, the 10.

Player Bets $5 on the come. ***The roll is a 7.*** While the 7 is a $5 winner for the new come bet, it is a loser for the two established points, and they are removed from the layout by the dealer.

The roll of the 7 cleared the layout, and the following roll will be a new come-out roll.

Don't Come Bets

Like the don't pass wager, a 7 or 11 on the first roll following a don't come bet is an automatic loser and the 2 and 3 are automatic winners, 12 being a standoff. (In casinos where the 2 is a standoff and the 12 a winner on the don't pass, the same will hold true for the don't come bets.)

If a 4, 5, 6, 8, 9 or 10 is thrown, establishing a point for the don't come bet, the dealer will move the chips behind the appropriate point box to mark the don't come point. Don't come bettors now win by having the 7 thrown before that point is made. Other numbers, as with the don't pass bets, are neutral rolls. Only the 7 and the come point determine the bet.

Let's follow a progression where the wrong bettor makes both don't pass and don't come bets.

Player Bets $5 on the don't pass. *The roll is a 10*, establishing 10 as the point.

Player Bets $5 on the don't come, continuing to bet against the dice. *The roll is a 2*, a $5 winner on the new don't come bet, and that bet is paid off and removed.

Player Bets $5 on the don't come. *The roll is a 6*. The dealer moves the bet from the don't come area to the upper section of the box numbered 6 to indicate that 6 is the point for this don't come bet. The player now has two points working, the 10 and 6, and decides to establish a third point.

Player Bets $5 on the don't come. *The roll is a 10*, a $5 loser on the don't pass since the point repeated before a 7 was thrown. The don't come point of 6 is unaffected, and the new don't come bet is moved to the 10 box, since 10 is the come point for the new don't come wager.

The player decides not to make any more bets, but if he did, he would bet don't pass for the next throw is a come-out roll. *The roll is 7*, winner on both come points, and they are paid off and removed. The next roll will be a new come-out roll.

Free-Odds Bets

Though not indicated anywhere on the layout, the **free-odds** or **odds** bets are the best bets a player can make at craps, and are an indispensable part of any winning strategy. The free-odds bets are so named, for, unlike the other bets at craps, the house has no advantage over the player. Hence, the term *free-odds*.

However, to make a free-odds bet, the player must first have placed a pass, don't pass, come or don't come wager, and in a sense, is backing those bets, for the free-odds bet can only be made in conjunction with these wagers.

When backed by single odds, the overall odds of the pass, don't pass, come and don't come bets drop to 0.8%, and where double odds are allowed and utilized, the overall odds drop to only 0.6% against the player.

The free odds wagers are the best odds a player can get at craps.

Free-Odds - Pass Line

Once a point is established on the come-out roll, the pass line bettor can make a **free-odds bet**. This is a bet that the pass line bettor's point will repeat before a 7 is thrown. In other words, if a 6 was established as his point, then that 6 would need to be thrown again before the 7 was rolled.

This bet is paid off at the correct odds, giving the house no edge, and is made by placing the chips behind the pass line wager and just outside the pass line area.

Pass Line and Free-Odds Bet

When single odds are allowed, the player can bet up to the amount wagered on his pass line bet, and in certain instances he can bet more.

And when double odds are allowed, the player can bet twice his pass line bet as a free-odds wager.

Though the player can bet less than the permissible amount on the free-odds wager and is allowed to reduce or remove this bet at any time, he should never do so, for the free-odds bets are the most advantageous bets in craps, and should be fully taken advantage of.

Following is a table which shows the correct odds of the point repeating before a 7 is thrown and the house payoff. Note how the house takes no percentage advantage on these bets since the payoff is identical to the correct odds.

ODDS OF POINT REPEATING BEFORE A SEVEN		
Point Number	Correct Odds	House Payoff
4 or 10	2 to 1	2 to 1
5 or 9	3 to 2	3 to 2
6 or 8	6 to 5	6 to 5

The odds presented in this table are easy to figure for the only numbers that affect the free-odds bet are the point number, which is a winner, and the 7, which is a loser. All other throws are inconsequential.

There are three ways to roll a winning 4 or 10, and six ways to roll a losing 7, thus 2 to 1 is the correct odds on points 4 or 10. A 5 or 9 can be rolled four ways each against the same six ways of rolling a 7, thus the correct odds are 3 to 2 against the 5 or 9. A 6 or 8 can be made by five combinations, and again, since there are six ways to roll a losing 7, the correct odds are 6 to 5 against the 6 or 8.

Special Allowances - Single Odds Game

To make the payoffs easier, most casinos allow the player to make a single odds bet greater than his pass line (or come) bet in the following instances.

• With a pass line bet such as $5 or $25 and the point being a 5 or 9, the casino will allow the player to make an odds bet of $6 and $30 respectively behind the line. If the bet is won, the 3 to 2 payoff on the $6 free-odds bet would be $9, and on the $30 bet, $45.

Without this special allowance, the player would be unable to get the full correct odds on the $5 or $25 free-odds bet since the $1 or more minimum craps tables do not deal in half dollars.

• With a three unit bet such as $3 or $15, and the point being a 6 or 8, the casino allows a five unit free-odds bet behind the line thus permitting the player to take full advantage of the 6 to 5 payoff on points 6 and 8. In the above examples, $5 and $25 free-odds bets would be permitted, and if won, would pay the player $6 and $30 respectively.

A three unit bet translates to $3 for the $1 bettor, $15 for the $5 bettor, $30 for the $10 bettor, and so on. Any bet that can be divisible by three can be considered a three unit bet and be backed by the special allowance single odds bets.

A $30 bet on the pass line can be backed by only $30 if the point is a 5 or 9 since the 3 to 2 payoff can be made on this amount, but if the point is a 6 or an 8, can be backed by $50 (five unit special allowance).

If uncertain about the amounts you are allowed to bet, check with the dealer, and he'll let you know the permissible wager.

No special allowances are allowed when the 4 or 10 are points for they are easily paid off at 2 to 1 no matter the amount wagered.

On bets smaller than $5 with the point being a 6 or 8, single odds bets will not receive the full

6 to 5 payoff, and will be paid off at even-money only, for again, the craps tables do not stock units smaller than $1 chips.

THREE UNIT BET -
SINGLE ODDS SPECIAL ALLOWANCE

Basic Three Unit Bet	6 or 8 as Point
$3	$5 ($6)
$15	$25 ($30)
$30	$50 ($60)
$45	$75 ($90)
$75	$125 ($150)
$300	$500 ($600)

The first column, *Basic Three Unit Bet*, is what our standard pass and come bet is, while the second column shows the special allowance permitted when the point is 6 or 8. Numbers in parenthesis indicate the amount paid if the single odds bet is won. Note that this is only a partial listing of the basic three unit bets.

On bets larger than $5 but in unequal multiples of $5, the free-odds bet will be paid to the highest multiple of $5 at 6 to 5, and the remainder will be paid at even-money. Thus, a $12 odds bet on the 8 will yield a payoff of only $14, $12

on the first $10 (at 6 to 5), and even-money on
the unequal remainder of $2.

When the free-odds bets do not receive their
full payoff, the bet works to the disadvantage of
the player. Therefore, we recommend that pass
and come wagers be made in multiples of $3, for
this allows the player to take full advantage of
the special allowances and lowers the overall
house edge for the single odds game below 0.8%.

Double Odds - Pass Line

Double odds work just like single odds except that the player is allowed to bet double his
pass line bet as a free-odds wager. If $10 was bet
on the pass line and a 5 was established as the
point, the double odds game allows the player to
bet $20 as a free-odds wager and receive the same
correct 3 to 2 odds on that point, instead of only
being allowed a $10 free-odds bet as in the single
odds game.

Special Allowances - Double Odds Game

One special allowance to keep in mind in
double odds games. With a two unit bet on the
pass line and the point a 6 or 8, double odds

games allow the player to wager five units as a free-odds bet. Thus, with a $10 bet (two $5 unit chips), and the point a 6 or 8, a $25 double odds bet would be allowed. If won, the 6 to 5 payoff would bring $30 in winnings (six $5 chips, an easier payoff for the casino).

We recommend that players bet in multiples of two for it permits us to take advantage of the special five unit allowance when the point is a 6 or an 8. Any bet that can be divisible by two can be considered a two unit bet and be backed by the special five unit allowance if the point is a 6 or an 8.

TWO UNIT BET - DOUBLE ODDS SPECIAL ALLOWANCE

Basic Two Unit Bet	6 or 8 as Point	4, 5, 9 or 10 as Point
$2	$5 ($6)	$4
$10	$25 ($30)	$20
$20	$50 ($60)	$40
$30	$75 ($90)	$60
$50	$125 ($150)	$100
$200	$500 ($600)	$400

*The first column, Basic Two Unit Bet, is our standard pass and come bet. The second column is the special allowance bets permitted when the point is 6 or 8. The third column is the normal double odds allowance for points 4, 5, 9 and 10.

Numbers in parenthesis ( ) indicate the payoff if the double odds bet is won (at 6 to 5 payoff) when the point is 6 or 8. Other two unit bets are possible.

Free-Odds - Don't Pass

Once the point is established, don't pass bettors are allowed to make a free-odds bet that a 7 will be rolled before the point repeats. The bet is paid off at correct odds, the house enjoying no edge, and is made by placing the free-odds bet next to the don't pass wager in the don't pass box.

Don't Pass and Free-Odds Bet

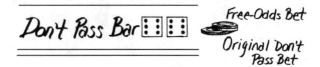

Since the odds favor the don't pass bettor once the point is established, there being more ways to roll a winning 7 than any point number, the don't pass bettor must *lay odds,* that is, put more money on the free-odds bet than he will win.

Let's say the point is a 4. The don't pass bettor's chances of winning the bet are now 2 to 1 in his favor. There are only three ways to roll a 4, a loser, against the six combinations of a 7, a winner. Therefore, the don't pass bettor must bet $20 to win $10 when the point is a 4 (or 10).

(On the other side of the bet, pass line bettors are receiving 2 to 1 odds, for their bet is the underdog, having only three winning chances against six losing combinations.)

To lay odds as a don't pass bettor, the allowable free-odds bet is determined by the *payoff,* not the original bet. Using the above example of a $10 bet on the don't pass with 4 established as the point, the don't pass bettor in a single odds game is allowed up to a $10 win on the free-odds bet.

Since the odds are 2 to 1 in his favor, the don't pass bettor must lay $20 to win $10. If it was a double odds game, meaning the player could win $20 on his original $10 bet, than at 1 to 2 odds, $40 would have to be staked for a potential win of $20.

The odds the don't pass bettor must lay are exactly opposite the odds pass line bettors take on the same points. Below is a table showing the free-odds bets from the wrong bettors position.

Like the free-odds bets for right bettors, don't pass free-odds wagers can be removed or reduced at any time, but since these are the player's best bets, it should not be done.

ODDS OF ROLLING A SEVEN BEFORE POINT REPEATS

Point Number	Correct Odds	House Payoff
4 or 10	1 to 2	1 to 2
5 or 9	2 to 3	2 to 3
6 or 8	5 to 6	5 to 6

Note how the house has no percentage advantage on these bets since the payoff is identical to the correct odds.

Let's look at a quick example to see how the free-odds bet works for the don't pass bettor.

$10 is bet on the don't pass, and the *come-out roll is a 9*. The wrong bettor *bets $15* behind the line as a free-odds bet, the maximum allowed in a single odds game. He stands to win $10 on the $15 free-odds bet if the 7 is rolled before the 9 repeats (since he's laying 2 to 3 odds), in addition to $10 on his don't pass bet.

Should the point be rolled before the 7, the $15 free-odds bet and $10 don't pass bet will be lost. If double odds were allowed, $20 would be the maximum allowable free-odds win. At 2 to 3 odds, the don't pass bettor would have to lay $30 to win that $20.

Wrong Bettors Special Allowances - Single Odds

The casino makes a special provision for don't pass bettors when the point is a 5 or 9 and an odd figure such as $5 is wagered. Since the craps tables do not deal in half dollars, the player is allowed to make a free-odds bet of $9 behind the line in this instance, and if the bet is won, will get paid $6 ($9 at 2 to 3).

When the point is 5 or 9 and the original bet is unequal, the house allows the player to bet more than the straight single odds. Just ask the dealer the exact amount allowed in those instances for the rules may vary from casino to casino.

Free-Odds: Come and Don't Come

Once a come point is established, the bettor can take odds (or lay odds for don't come bettors) and get the same advantageous payoffs, 2-1 on points 4 and 10 (1-2 for wrong bettors), 3-2 on the 5 and 9 (2-3), and 6-5 on the 6 and 8 (5-6). The same special allowances apply for these free-odds bets.

The house has no advantage on these wagers, and like the line bets, the overall house edge on the come or don't come bets teamed with single odds drops to 0.8%, and with double odds, to 0.6%.

However, the odds bets on the come and don't come bets are placed differently than line bets. Rather than being made by the player, the odds bets are given to the dealer to place with the instruction, "odds on the come," or "odds on the don't come."

The dealer will place the odds bet in the appropriate box atop the come point, but slightly offset, so that the odds bet can be differentiated from the come bet.

Come, Don't Come and Free-Odds Bets

					don't come and free-odds bet
4	5	SIX	8	NINE	10 come and free-odds bet

COME

Dealer will place free-odds bet atop
original bet but offset to distinguish from
come or don't come bet.

The only other difference is with the come
bet. While the come bet itself is working on the
come-out roll, the *odds bet on that come bet is
not*. Let's say the player had $15 bet on the come
point of 6 and had that bet backed by $25 free-
odds.

A come-out roll of a 7 would of course be a
loser for the $15 come bet, as that bet is always
working, but since the free-odds bet was off, the
$25 single odds wager would be returned to the
player.

If a 6 was rolled instead, a winner for the
come bet, the player would only win the $15, and
be returned the $25 odds bet.

Though it is standard procedure for the free-
odds bet backing the come wager to be off on the

come-out roll, the player can request the odds bet to be "on" by informing the dealer that the "odds are on for the come bet," and then, of course, the odds bet is subject to the normal rules.

The odds on the don't come bets, as with the pass and don't pass wagers, are always working.

THE REST OF THE BETS

With the exception of the place bet of 6 and 8, none of the bets presented in this section, which include the remainder of the bets possible at craps, are recommended for play. The house edge over the player on these bets is too large to be incorporated into a winning strategy, and the bettor making these bets will soon find himself drained of significant portions of his bankroll.

The bets listed in this section are discussed anyway so that you have a full understanding of all possibilities, and are never tempted to make these poor wagers.

Place Bets

The **place bets** are among the most popular wagers in craps, and are a bet that a particular point number, whichever is wagered on, the 4, 5, 6, 8, 9 or 10, is rolled before a 7 is thrown. The player can make as many place bets as he wants, and some players do, covering all the numbers with place bets.

However, this is not recommended strategy, for as we will see, with the exception of the place bets of 6 and 8, the other place bets, the 4, 5, 9 and 10, are poor wagers, and will have no role in our winning strategies.

Place bets are made by giving the dealer the desired wager, and telling him, for example, "to place the 9," or any such statement that indicates the player wants to make a place bet on the 9.

Though place bets can be made at any time, they are not working, or are "**off**" on the come-out roll, unless the player requests them to be "**on**" (working). The player can also request his place bets to be off for a limited series of throws, and may increase, reduce or remove them at any time prior to a roll.

HOUSE PAYOFFS ON PLACE BETS

Bet	Payoff	Correct Odds	House Edge
4 or 10	9 to 5	2 to 1	6.67%
5 or 9	7 to 5	3 to 2	4.00%
6 or 8	7 to 6	6 to 5	1.52%

To get the full payoffs on the place bets, the player should make his bets in the proper multiples. On place bets of 4 and 10, and 5 and 9, the bets should be made in multiples of $5 since the payoffs are 9 to 5 and 7 to 5 respectively. On the 6 and 8, the bet should be in multiples of $6 (7 to 6 payoff).

Excess bets in unequal multiples will be paid off at even-money only and work to the disadvantage of the player. For example, a $10 bet on the 6 will be paid as follows. The first $6 will get the full 7 to 6 odds for $7, while the remaining $4 gets paid at even-money, or $4, for a total win of $11. The last $4, paid off at only even-money, is a terrible payoff, and makes the entire bet a poor one.

Unless the player makes the place bets of 6 or 8 in multiples of $6 to insure full payoffs, the bet should not be made. Also, bets less than $5 on the 4, 5, 9 and 10, and less than $6 on the 6 and 8, will be paid of at only even-money.

To summarize, do not make place bets of 4 or 10, or 5 and 9, for the house edge is too high.

The place bets of 6 and 8 have playable odds of 1.52% and can be used in an aggressive maximize gain strategy, though some players may prefer to stick with the line, come and don't come bets backed by free-odds, the best bets of all.

Big 6 and Big 8

The **Big 6** and **Big 8** are bets that a particular number bet on, the 6 or 8, is thrown before a 7 is rolled. These bets can be made at any time, and are bet by putting the wager into the box marked Big 6 or Big 8.

These bets work just like the place bets of 6 and 8 except that the house only pays even-money on a won bet as opposed to the 7 to 6 payoff he would receive had he made the superior place bet on 6 or 8 instead. The house has a whopping 9.90% advantage on the Big 6 and Big 8 bets.

Buying the 4 or 10

This is an option the casino gives the player when betting on a place number, and though it reduces the odds on the 4 or 10 from 6.67% to 4.76%, the buy bet is still a poor one and should not be made. But here's how it works.

To **buy** the 4 or 10, you must give the house a 5% commission on your bet. Once you've bought a number, the house will pay off the bet at the correct odds. Thus, your payoff will be 2 to 1, the correct odds, rather than 9 to 5 as is usually the payoff for these place bets.

A 5% commission on $20 would be $1. For any bet smaller than $20, the commission would still be $1 since the craps tables generally carry no smaller units. In these cases, the house edge on your buy bet would be much larger than 4.76%. If you buy the 4 and 10 at $10 each, for a total of $20, the commission would only be 5% of the two bet total, or $1.

Like the place bets, buy bets are not working on the come-out roll, unless you instruct the dealer that the bet is on. They are also similar to the place bets in that they can be increased, reduced or removed at any time prior to the roll. Note that an increased buy bet is subject to the 5% commission on the additional wager.

Some casinos will keep the 5% commission if you decide to remove an established bet or charge an additional 5% if you win your bet and decide to let it ride.

Buying the 5, 6, 8, 9

Theoretically, you can buy these numbers as well, but since the commission is 5%, and the house edge on all these place bets is less than that, there is no advantage in buying these numbers.

Lay Bets

The **lay bet** is the opposite of a buy bet, and is used by wrong bettors who are wagering that the 7 will be thrown before the point or points they bet against is rolled. While the bet is paid off at correct odds, it costs the bettor 5% commission on the projected win to get this payoff, and is therefore, a poor bet.

Lay bets, which can be added to, reduced or removed altogether at any time, are made by giving the dealer your chips along with the required 5% commission on the projected win. The dealer will place the bet above the point number covered (in the area where the don't come bets are placed) and place a buy button on top to distinguish the lay bet.

To receive the full value on the lay bet of 4 or 10, the bettor would have to wager at least $40 to win $20 (1 to 2 odds). The 5% commission on the projected win of $20 would be $1. Any bet smaller than the $40 lay bet on the 4 or 10 would still be charged the minimum $1 commission (craps tables do not generally deal in currency smaller than $1 chips) making the house edge greater than the 2.44% advantage already built into this wager.

The 5 and 9 lay bets would require a minimum wager of $30 for the player to get the maximum value. The potential $20 win (laying odds at 2 to 3) would be charged $1 commission. The 6 and 8 bets would require a wager of $24 at 5 to 6 odds on a projected win of $20 to get full value from the commission. Any bet smaller than the projected win of $20 would still be charged the minimum $1 commission, and raise the overall house edge on the wager.

HOUSE ALLOWANCE ON LAY BETS	
Points	House Advantage
4 or 10	2.44%
5 or 9	3.23%
6 or 8	4.00%

Field Bet

The **field bet** is a one roll wager that the next throw of the dice will be a number listed in the field box, the 2, 3, 4, 9, 10, 11 or 12. If one of the numbers not listed is rolled, the 5, 6, 7 or 8, then the bet is lost.

The field bet can be made at any time and is done by placing the wager in the area marked "Field".

At first glance, the bet seems attractive. There are seven winning numbers listed in the field box, and two of these numbers, the 2 and the 12, pay double if they are rolled. In some casinos, the 2 or 12 pays triple. The other winning numbers, the 3, 4, 9, 10 and 11 pay even-money.

However, there are 20 combinations (of the 5, 6, 7 and 8) that will beat us, and only 16 that will win, giving the house an edge of 5.55% when the 2 and 12 are paid at 2 to 1, and 2.70% when one is paid at 2 to 1 and the other at 3 to 1.

Proposition, or Center Bets

The **proposition**, or **center bets**, as they are sometimes called, are located at the center of the layout, and are made by either giving the chips to the dealer who will pass them along to the stickman, or, as with the hardways bet or craps-eleven bet, can sometimes be tossed directly to the stickman.

The central area of the layout is under the complete domain of the stickman, and though he will physically handle the placing and removing of bets in this area, it is with the dealer that the player will generally make his bets and receive his payoffs.

The proposition bets are the worst bets a player can make at craps and should never be made. The house advantage rages as high as 16.67% on some of these wagers. However, these bets are listed and their odds explained so that the reader will be fully conversant with all the wagers possible at craps.

Any Seven

This bet that the following roll of the dice will be a 7, is paid off by the house at 4 to 1 (5 for 1), and is among the worst bets a player can make. The house maintains an exorbitant edge of 16.67% over the player. Don't even make this bet in your dreams.

Any Craps

This bet, located at the bottom of the center layout and along its sides, is a bet that the following roll will be a craps - a 2, 3 or 12.

There are four ways to roll a winner. The 2 and 12 account for one way each, while there are two ways to roll a three. The other 32 combinations are losers, making the correct odds 8 to 1. The house only pays 7 to 1, giving them an 11.1% advantage.

2 or 12

This is a bet that the next roll of the dice will come up a 2, or a 12 if you bet that number, and is paid off by the house at 30 to 1. Of the 36 possible combinations of the dice, there is only one way of rolling a 2 or a 12, making the correct odds 35 to 1 against rolling either number.

With only a 30 to 1 payoff, the house enjoys a hefty 13.69% advantage.

Sometimes a casino may only pay off at 30 for 1 (29 to 1), giving them an edge of 16.67%. This should make no difference to us for we won't go near that bet in either case.

3 or 11

This is a wager that the following roll will be a 3, or an 11, whichever you place your money on, and the house payoff is 15 to 1. Since there are only 2 ways to roll either number out of a possible 36 combinations, the correct odds are 17 to 1 (34 losers, 2 winners). The house edge is 11.1%. Where the payoff is 15 for 1 (14 to 1), this edge jumps to 16.67%.

Horn Bet

It takes four chips or multiples thereof to makes this bet. The horn bet is a four way bet that the next roll will be a 2, 3, 11 or 12, in effect combining four poor bets together. The house pays off the winning number at the normal pay-offs (15 to 1 for the 3 or 11, and 30 to 1 for the 2 or 12), and deducts the other three losing chips from the payoff.

This sucker bet combines four losing wagers for a combined house edge of 11.1%, or 16.67% with the poorer payoffs discussed earlier. Never make this bet.

Hop Bet

This one roll wager, which does not appear on the layout, is generally made on a combination of the dice not otherwise offered on the one roll bets, such as 2, 3. If the bet is a pair such as 5, 5, the player will get the same payoff as the casino gives on the 2 or 12 bet (30 to 1 or 29 to 1). If the bet is a non-pair, such as 4, 5, which has two ways to win (4, 5; 5, 4), the payoff will be the same as on the 3 or 11 bet (15 to 1 or 14 to 1).

To make a hop bet, give your bet to the dealer or stickman, and call out for example "Hop 54", if the 5, 4 is the hop bet you wish to make. With the more generous payoff hop bets give the casino an edge of 13.39%, otherwise the edge is 16.67%. In either case, consider the bet a donation to the casino.

Craps-Eleven

The stickman will constantly exhort the player to make this horrendous bet, which is an appeal to bet the Any Craps and 11 bet simultaneously. We don't want to go near either bet by itself let alone together. Save your money for the show.

Hardways

Whenever the numbers, 4, 6, 8 or 10 are rolled as doubles, the roll is said to be thrown **hardways**. A throw of 2-2 is said to be **4, the hardway** or **hard 4**, and similarly with 3-3, 4-4 and 5-5 for hard 6, 8 and 10 respectively. Rolling the 4, 6, 8 and 10 in other combinations is called **easy** such as 6-4; *10 the easy way*.

Betting hardways is betting that the particular number you choose comes up hard before it comes up easy or before a 7 is thrown.

Hard 4 and Hard 10

There is only one way to throw a hard 4 (2-2) or hard 10 (5-5), and eight ways to lose - six ways to roll a seven, and two ways to throw a 4 or 10 the easy way (1-3, 3-1, 6-4 and 4-6). The correct odds are 8 to 1 but the house only pays 7 to 1 for an advantage of 11.1%. This weak bet should never be made.

Hard 6 and Hard 8

There are a total of 10 losing combinations - the 6 ways to roll a 7, and 4 ways to roll a 6 or an 8 the easy way. There is only 1 way to throw the 6 or 8 the hardway. The correct odds of this hardway bet is 10 to 1 but the house only pays 9 to 1, a hefty 9.09% edge.

WINNING STRATEGIES:
BETTING WITH THE DICE

We'll use only the best bets in our strategies - the pass line, come and free-odds wagers, wagers which give the player the best chances of winning, and lower the house edge to 0.8% in single odds games and 0.6% in double odds ones.

Built-in to the strategies are methods to turn average wins into big winning sessions without any risk of big losses.

Basic Conservative Strategy -
Single Odds

Our standard bet will be in increments of three units so that we can take advantage of the special free-odds allowances should the points be 6 or 8, whereupon we can back our pass line or come bet by five units, or points 5 or 9, where we can bet extra if the original bet is uneven such as $15, where $20 would be permitted as a free-odds wager.

This allows maximum usage of the free-odds bets, wagers the house has no edge on, and brings the overall house advantage down to the barest minimum possible in a single odds game.

These are the guidelines of the **Basic Conservative Strategy:**

• We will make three unit pass line and come bets until we have two points established, and back both those bets with the maximum single odds allowed.

• Every time a point repeats, whether as a come or pass line point, we will make another three unit pass line or come bet so that we continue to have two points working for us. If a 2, 3, 11 or 12 declares a winner or a loser on the new pass line or come bet, we will follow with another bet until we get that second point established and then take the maximum single odds allowed on that point.

• If the shooter sevens-out, clearing the board of all bets, we'll begin the progression again with a new pass line bet.

Aggressive Strategy - Single Odds

Rather than playing only two points as in the **Basic Conservative Strategy**, this method immediately attempts to establish three points. Otherwise, all the principles and methods are the same.

With three points covered, the bettor using the **Aggressive Strategy** can make a lot of money when the shooter starts rolling numbers.

Double Odds Strategies

Whenever the bettor has a choice, he should always choose a double odds game over a single odds game, for the additional allowance of the free-odds bet drops the overall house edge from 0.8% to 0.6% when using our methods.

The playing strategies we will pursue in the double odds game are identical to the single odds game except that we will bet in units of two instead of units of three as recommended in the single odds game to take advantage of the special five unit free-odds allowance when the point is 6 or 8.

Basic Conservative Strategy bettors should establish two points with maximum double odds, while **Aggressive Strategy** bettors will want to cover three points. Follow the procedures for the single odds methods substituting only the two unit basic bet for the three unit bet, and making double odds bets instead of single odds.

Maximizing Profits - Double Odds Game

Again our strategy here will follow that of the single odds game except we'll be increasing our bets by two units instead of three.

Basic Conservative Strategy bettors won't begin increasing bets until they've accumulated 20 units in profits, and Aggressive bettors will need 25 units. Remember to take advantage of the special allowances when the point is a 6 or 8. A four unit bet can be backed by 10 units in the double odds game, and a six unit bet by 15.

When eventually the shooter sevens-out, ending our winning streak, we'll start the next progression again at two units, ready to capitalize on another hot roll should one develop.

WINNING STRATEGIES: BETTING AGAINST THE DICE

Though the odds of winning are equivalent to the right betting strategies, 0.8% in a single odds game and 0.6% in a double odds game, very few craps players bet against the dice. Many bettors feel uncomfortable about having to *lay odds*, putting more money on their free-odds bet than they'll win, but as stated earlier, the free-odds wagers give the house no edge betting right or wrong.

However, players betting against the dice don't mind laying odds, for the roll of a 7, their winner, will occur more often than any point number, and they'll have frequent winners.

In addition, should a point be repeated, a losing roll for wrong bettors, only one bet will be lost. The other points covered by the wrong bettor are still in play. On the other side of the dice, the right bettors fear the 7, for when it is thrown - boom - all their established points and free-odds bets are lost.

We will apply the same principles of play as right bettors. We'll make only the best bets available to us, those that reduce the house edge to the lowest possible figure - the don't pass, the don't come and free-odds bets.

Basic Conservative Strategy
Single Odds Wrong Bettors

Our standard bet will be in even increments of two units. Bets such as $15 or $25 are difficult to work with when the point is a 5 or 9 and 2 to 3 odds should be laid. Betting in other unit sizes is equally valid, but the player will find it easiest to work in multiples of $10.

These are the guidelines of the **Basic Conservative Strategy:**

• We will make two unit don't pass and don't come bets until we have established bets against two points, and back both those bets with maximum free-odds.

• Should a point repeat, a loser for us, we will make another don't come or don't pass bet, so that we can continue to have bets working against two points. If a 2, 3, 11 or 12 determines a winner or loser on a new don't pass or don't come bet, we will follow with another bet until we get that second point established, and then we'll play the maximum single odds against that point.

• Stop establishing don't pass and don't come bets if a second point repeats. This is an important safeguard to protect us against bad losing streaks.

• If a 7 is thrown, a winner on all our bets, we'll begin the progression again with our two unit don't pass bet.

As cautious bettors, we'll limit ourselves to only two points and strictly follow the safeguards recommended in step 3.

Aggressive Strategy Single Odds Wrong Bettors

Our **Aggressive Strategy** follows the same guidelines as the **Basic-Conservative Strategy** except that we'll cover three points during a shoot instead of two, and will stop making additional don't pass and don't come bets if three points repeat, instead of two as advised in the **Basic Conservative Strategy**.

We'll use the same bets - the don't pass, don't come and free-odds bets, and enjoy the same low 0.8% house edge as in a single odds game.

Double Odds Strategy - Wrong Bettors

Whenever possible, the wrong bettor should play a double odds game over a single odds game, for it lowers the overall house edge from 0.8% to 0.6%.

And we always want to play with the best odds we can get - the lower the house edge, the greater our chances of winning.

By nature, the double odds strategies are more aggressive than the single odds games, and are more in tune for players whose temperament demands hotter action. The double odds bettor lays more to win more and therefore needs a larger bankroll than his single odds counterpart. Therefore, to play this strategy, the double odds bettor must feel comfortable with the larger bet levels.

Our double odds strategies are identical to the single odds methods, except that we're playing double odds instead of single odds. We'll begin by making a two unit don't pass bet, and backing that bet by double odds once a point is established.

Basic Conservative Strategy bettors will follow with a don't come bet and lay double odds on both points while **Aggressive Strategy** bettors will make two more don't come bets backed by the full double odds.

Like the single odds strategies, **Basic Conservative Strategy** players attempt to keep two points working at all times while **Aggressive Strategy** players strive for three working points.

When points repeat, new don't pass or don't come bets are made to reestablish another point, but should a second point repeat for **Basic Conservative Strategy** players or a third point for **Aggressive Strategy** players, then we'll curtail all new betting until the shooter sevens-out, a winner on our remaining bets.

We employ this stop-loss as a safeguard to protect against one really bad shoot wiping out our table stakes. However, should the dice start blowing profits in our direction, we're immediately ready to capitalize on the situation.

We start the next come-out roll fresh, with a two unit don't pass wager, always ready for the streak that will mint chips for us.

WINNING AT ROULETTE

INTRODUCTION

Roulette offers the player a huge variety of bets, more than any other casino table game, and the constant possibilities of winning and the different payoffs of the wagers, ranging from even-money payoffs to returns of 35 to 1, keeps the game exciting and suspenseful.

We'll show you how to make all the different bets possible in roulette, the odds involved and how the game is played both here and abroad so that you'll be ready to play roulette anywhere in the world and be fully prepared to win!

THE BASICS OF ROULETTE
The Roulette Wheel

Roulette is played with a circular wheel containing 36 grooved slots numbered from 1 to 36, half the numbers of which are black and the other half red, a tiny ball which is used in conjunction with the wheel, and a betting layout where players can place their wagers.

In addition to the 36 numbers on the roulette wheel, the American game has a 0 and 00, while the European game has but one 0. The zero slots are neither red nor black as are the other numbers but are green in color.

The American Wheel

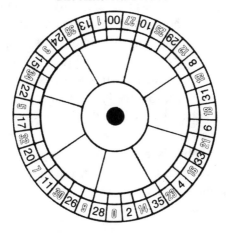

The wheel is cut into tiny pockets, one for each number - 37 total on a European wheel and 38 on an American - so that the ball, when spun around the wheel, will eventually fall into one of these slots - that number being the winning spin.

The Layout

The European game generally has the wheel flanked on two sides by a betting layout, so that the busy tables can accommodate players on both sides of the wheel, while the less popular American games use but one layout to the side.

The Dealer

The American game typically employs just one dealer who handles all of the functions at the table. He changes money into chips, spins the wheel, collects losing bets and pays off the winners. In between he finds time to stack and restack collected chips from the layout into neat, colorful piles, so that payoffs from the next spin will proceed smoothly and rapidly.

If a table is exceptionally busy, the dealer may have an assistant to help run the game and handle the action.

WINNING AT ROULETTE

European style games have one to as many as three or four **croupiers**, the French term for dealers, paying and collecting bets on the two adjacent layouts, and a **tourneur**, whose main responsibility is to spin the wheel and call the result. Often, a supervisor will be present as well.

Thus, when things get rolling and the tables crowded, one might find as many as six casino personnel manning a roulette game - a tourneur, four croupiers and a supervisor.

The Roulette Layout

		0		00	
1to18	1st 12	1	2	3
		4	5	6
EVEN		7	8	9
		10	11	12
◇	2nd 12	13	14	15
		16	17	18
◆		19	20	21
		22	23	24
ODD	3rd 12	25	26	27
		28	29	30
19to36		31	32	33
		34	35	36
		2-1	2-1	2-1

WINNING AT ROULETTE

The Play of the Game

Once players have placed their bets on the layout, choosing from the myriad possibilities available in front of them, the game is officially ready to begin. The roulette wheel will be spun by the dealer or tourneur who immediately afterwards, will throw the ball in the opposite direction from which the wheel is spinning so that both ball and wheel are racing in opposite directions on the wheel itself.

Players must now get in their last minute wagers for when the ball is about to leave the track, the dealer will announce that bets are no longer permitted. The call of *Faites vos jeux, messieurs* (Make your bets gentlemen) or *Rien ne va plus* (Nothing more goes) are classic in the French speaking casinos.

Once the ball has stopped, the dealer or tourneur will call out the outcome, and a marker will be placed on the number just spun so that all players and dealers can clearly see the winning number.

The dealers or **croupiers**, as they're called in French, will now settle the wagers. Lost bets are collected first by the dealers, and after this is done, all the winning bets will be paid off.

The Chips

Keeping track of one's bets are easy in American roulette games, for each player is issued special chips applicable only to the roulette game at that casino, and these chips are colored, a different color for each player. Ten different players may be represented by, for example, yellow, red, pink, blue, green, black, white, beige, purple and grey chips.

The colored chips are valid and can be used only at the roulette table which issues them. If the table is crowded and no more colors are available, a player may use regular casino chips for his or her bets.

There is no confusion in ownership of the chips this way. Color coding makes life easy at these tables. When a player approaches the roulette table, he exchanges cash or casino chips for an equivalent value in the colored chips, called in the parlance of the game, **wheel checks**. The value assigned to those colored chips, be it 25¢, $1.00, $5.00 or whatever, is set by the player. Thus, if the player wants to value the chips at 25¢, more chips will be issued from the dealer than if the chips were valued at $1.00.

The dealer will place a coin or **marker button** on top of the colored chips and place these on the stationary outer rim of the wheel, so that the value of that wheel check is clearly marked.

When a player is ready to leave, he converts the wheel checks back into the regular casino checks with the dealer at that table.

Life is a bit more complicated in the European style game where color coding is not used and bettors simply use casino chips or cash to make their bets. Sometimes, in the confusion of a crowded game, vociferous arguments ensue as players lay identical claim to chips on the felt.

The Basic Odds

The primary difference in the popularity of European and American roulette lies in the simple fact that the European game gives the player much better odds of winning, and this is where the 0, 00 difference of the two wheels comes into play.

Let's see how the odds are figured.

There are slots numbered from 1 to 36 on the roulette wheel - a total of 36. There is only one way to win for each number chosen. That leaves 35 other numbers, which if they come up, are losers for the bettor. True odds of 35 to 1 against - 35 ways to lose, one way to win.

And that's exactly what the casino will pay on a single number bet.

So where is the casino's profit?

It is the zeros added to the wheel that give casinos their edge, for now there are a total of 37 possibilities on a European wheel (single zero added) and 38 possibilities on an American one (double zero added). The casino's payoff is still 35 to 1, being based on the true odds of a 36 number wheel. However, with the added zeros, the true odds on a single number bet are now 36 to 1 on a single zero wheel (the European game) and 37 to 1 on a double zero wheel (the American game).

Those zeros give the casino its edge on all bets made. Unless the zero (and in American roulette the 00 also) are bet directly, the spin of either on the wheel causes all other wagers to lose.

The sole exceptions are the even-money bets in a European style game (and Atlantic City), for the spin of a zero gives the red-black (rouge-noir), high-low (passe-manque) and odd-even (impair-pair) bettors a second chance, and reduces the house edge on these bets to 1.35% (2.63% in Atlantic City) - the best odds one can receive in roulette.

The zeros represent the house advantage and that is why the 00 in American roulette makes that game a worse gamble for the player than its European counterpart. Atlantic City makes up for this a little by offering surrender on even-money bets, bringing the casino's edge on these wagers down to 2.63%.

Let's sum up the odds for you in chart form so that you can clearly see them in one spot.

CASINO EDGE IN ROULETTE

American Roulette (Double Zero)	House Edge
The 5-Number Bet	7.89%
All Other Bets	5.26%
Atlantic City - Even Money Bets	2.63%
European Roulette (One Zero)	
Even-Money Bets - En Prison Rule	1.35%
All Other Bets	2.70%

The difference between the 1.35% of European style roulette and 5.26% of the American style is significant, almost a four-fold increase, which calculates directly to a loss rate four times as fast.

Now you can see why roulette with a single zero and en prison rule is the rage of Europe, and double zero American roulette is less popular.

THE BETS

Roulette offers the player a multitude of possible wagers, more than any other casino table game. All in all, there are over 150 possible combinations to bet. A player may make as many bets in whatever combinations desired as long as the bets fit within the minimum and maximum limit of the casino.

Let's now examine the bets one by one. (The French terms for the bets are listed in the parenthesis.)

Combination or Inside Bets

These bets are made within the numbers on the layout, and hence, are termed *inside bets*.

Single Number Bet - (En Plein)

A **single number bet** can be made on any number on the layout including the 0 and 00. To make this wager, place your chip within the lines of the number chosen, being careful not to touch the lines. Otherwise you may have another bet altogether.

The winning payoff is 35 to 1.

The Single Number Bet

Split Bet (A Cheval)

Place the chip on the line adjoining two numbers. If either number comes up, the payoff is 17 to 1.

Split Bet (A Cheval)

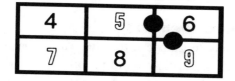

Trio Bet (Transversale)

The chip is placed on the outside vertical line alongside any line of numbers. If any of the three are hit, the payoff is 11 to 1.

Trio Bet (Transversale)

4-Number Bet (Carre)

Also called a square or corner bet. Place the chip on the spot marking the intersection of four numbers. If any of the four come in it is an 8 to 1 payoff.

4-Number Bet (Carre)

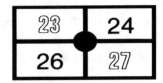

Quatre Premiere

Only in European roulette. The bet covering the 0, 1, 2 and 3. An 8 to 1 payoff.

5-Number Bet

Only in American roulette. Place the chip at the intersection of the 0, 00 and 2 to cover those numbers plus the 1 and 3. If any of these five come home, the payoff is 6 to 1. In American roulette, it is the only bet not giving the house an edge of 5.26%. It's worse - 7.89%!

5-Number Bet

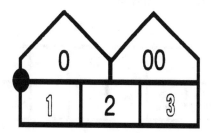

6-Number Bet (Sixaine)

Also called a **block bet**. The chip should be put on the outside line of the layout while intersecting the line separating the sets of numbers chosen. The payoff is 5 to 1.

6-Number Bet (Sixaine)

28	29	30
31	32	33

Outside Bets

These bets are outside the 36 numbers on the layout, and are aptly called, the outside bets. These include the columns, dozens and even money bets - red-black, high-low and odd-even.

Outside Bets

1st 12		2nd 12		3rd 12	
1to18	EVEN	◇	◆	ODD	19to36

Columns Bet (Colonne)

A chip placed at the head of a column, on the far side from the zero or zeros, covers all 12 numbers in the column and has a winning payoff of 2 to 1. The 0 and 00 are not included in this bet and would be a loser if they come up.

Columns Bet (Colonne)

3	6	9	12	15	18	21	24	27	30	33	36	2-1
2	5	8	11	14	17	20	23	26	29	32	35	2-1
1	4	7	10	13	16	19	22	25	28	31	34	2-1

Dozens Bet (Douzaine)

This is another way to bet 12 numbers, either numbers 1 to 12, 13 to 24 or 25 to 36. On the American layout they're called the **first**, **second** and **third dozen** respectively, and on the French layout, they're known as **P12**, **M12** and **D12**. The winning payoff as in the column bet is 2 to 1.

Dozens Bet (Douzaine)

1st 12 ●	2nd 12 ●	3rd 12 ●

Even-Money Bets

There is one final type of bet, the even money bets: **Red-Black** (Rouge-Noir), **High-Low** (Passe-Manque) and **Odd-Even** (Impair-Pair). Spots for these bets are found outside the numbers, thus classified as *outside wagers*.

These wagers are clearly marked in large boxes.

In Atlantic City and European style roulette, these bets are the best at the roulette table, for they offer the player additional features which are greatly advantageous. In Europe, the features are called *en prison* and *partage*, and in Atlantic City, *surrender*.

Even-Money Bets

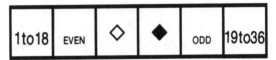

Red-Black (Rouge-Noir)

There are 18 black and 18 red numbers. A player may bet either the **red** or the **black** and is paid off at 1 to 1 on a winning spin.

Red-Black (Rouge-Noir)

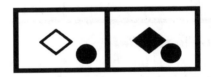

High-Low (Passe-Manque)

Numbers 1-18 may be bet (**low**) or 19-36 (**high**). Bets are paid off at 1 to 1.

High-Low (Passe-Manque)

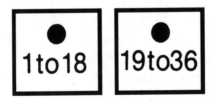

Odd-Even (Impair-Pair)

A player may bet on the 18 even numbers (**even**) or on the 18 odd numbers (**odd**). Winning bets are paid at 1 to 1.

Odd-Even (Impair-Pair)

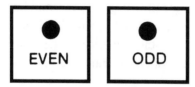

En Prison and Partage

It is on these even number bets - Red-Black, High-Low and Odd-Even - where the American and European games really differ. In American roulette, the house automatically wins on these bets when the 0 or 00 is spun (except in Atlantic City). However, in Europe, if the 0 is spun, the **en prison** rule comes into effect. The player has two choices now.

He or she can either surrender half the bet, called **partage**, or elect to allow the bet to be "imprisoned" one more spin. If the spin is won, the bet stays intact and is "released" for the player to do what he or she will. If the spin is lost, so is the bet.

This rule is greatly advantageous to the player, and brings the odds down on these bets to 1.35% in favor of the casino as opposed to the 2.70% on the rest of the bets in the single zero game.

Surrender

In an attempt to get more gamblers to play roulette, the game in Atlantic City helps make up for the 00 of the American wheel by offering **surrender**, which is really partage by another name.

When a 0 or 00 is spun, players with bets on any of the even-money propositions lose only half the bet, "surrendering it," and keep the other half. This brings the house edge down to 2.63% on these bets.

American and European Roulette

The European and American game is pretty much the same besides the use of the French terms in Europe, and of course the American terms in the U.S. casinos.

However, there are two significant differences.

• In addition to the 36 numbers on the roulette wheel, the American game has a 0 and 00, while the European game has but one 0.

WINNING AT ROULETTE

- The European game offers en prison and partage, rules greatly beneficial to the player. En prison and partage is not offered in American casinos, with the exception of Atlantic City where surrender (partage) is used.

The end result, as we showed earlier, is that the casino edge in the European game is but 1.35% as opposed to American roulette where the player has to overcome a hefty 5.26% house edge (or 2.63% on even-money bets in Atlantic City).

WINNING STRATEGIES

First it must be stated clearly, that like most other casino games, the casino has the mathematical edge over the player, and that no betting strategy or playing system can overcome those odds unless the wheel is a biased one - which we'll cover.

That edge is 5.26% in American roulette, with the exception of even-money bets in Atlantic City where the edge is 2.63%, and 2.70% in European roulette, unless the even-money wagers are made, where the house edge drops to 1.35%.

Based on the above facts, one must develop a clear picture on how to approach a winning strategy.

ROULETTE PAYOFF CHART

Bets in Roulette

American Name	#	French Name	Payoff
Single Number	1	En Plein	35 - 1
Split Bet	2	A Cheval	17 - 1
Trio	3	Transversale	11 - 1
4-Number (Corner)	4	Carre	8 - 1
(Not Applicable)	4	Quatre Premiere	8 - 1
5-Number	5	(Not Applicable)	6 - 1
6-Number or Block	6	Sixaine	5 - 1
Columns Bet	12	Colonne	2 - 1
Dozens Bet	12	Dozaine	2 - 1
Red or Black	18	Rouge ou Noir	1 - 1
High or Low	18	Passe ou Manque	1 - 1
Odd or Even	18	Impair ou Pair	1 - 1

 # column is the amount of numbers covered by the bet.

First of all, it must be understood that in the long haul, the casino's edge will grind out the player - but that doesn't mean the player can't show a profit in the short run. Fluctuations are normal to gambling, whatever the game, and with a little luck, a player can ride a hot streak into some healthy profits.

There are many betting systems that have been devised to overcome the casino's edge in roulette, but you must keep these in perspective, for they can no more alter or change the built-in house edge than one constantly calling a tree a river will change that tree to a river or calling blue red will change blue to red.

This is not to say that some of the betting strategies don't look good - some of them are brilliant in concept and *appear* foolproof. As long as one realizes the risks involved and understands that no strategy can negate the built-in house edge, betting strategies can be a lot of fun.

Betting strategies can work - in the short run - and provide the player with a fun, working approach to winning, and really, that's what the game is all about.

Let's look at one of the most famous systems first, The Martingale.

The Martingale

This dangerous system can dig you into a deep hole quick should you have a long string of losses - if not, like other systems, you'll be sitting pretty.

The system is easy. You attempt to win $1.00 on every sequence of the wheel, a sequence being defined as either one spin when you have won, or a number of spins, ending when there is a winner.

Your first bet is $1.00. If the bet is won, you start again, betting $1.00. If you lose, the bet is doubled to $2.00. Should that bet be won, you have won $1.00 on the sequence, a $1.00 loss on the first spin a a $2.00 win on the second. If the second bet is lost, the next bet is again doubled, and is now $4.00. A winner here again brings a $1.00 profit, $1.00 + $2.00 in losers for $3.00 total, and a $4.00 winner. Still $1.00 over the top.

And so the system works. Every won bet is followed by a $1.00 wager, the beginning of a fresh cycle. Every lost bet is followed by a doubling of that bet. And here is the danger of the Martingale. As consecutive losses mount, so does the size of your bet, where the end result is only a $1.00 win!

This is what happens if you lose seven in a row.

MARTINGALE PROGRESSION		
Loss	**Bet**	**Total Loss**
1st	$1.00	$1.00
2nd	$2.00	$3.00
3rd	$4.00	$7.00
4th	$8.00	$15.00
5th	$16.00	$31.00
6th	$32.00	$63.00
7th	$64.00	$127.00
8th	$128.00	-

Now suddenly, you're faced with a $128.00 bet with $127.00 worth of losses behind you. Now that's a lot of sweat and aggravation just to win $1.00 on the sequence. And we all know that seven losses in a row is not that strange of an occurrence.

What happens on the next spin? Surely you're due for a winner now after seven consecutive losses. If you're pregnant or expecting a raise or some such thing, you may be due.

In gambling, you're never due for anything. There are expectations based on the odds, but the fact that seven times the wheel spun black when you've been betting red, has no bearing on the eighth spin. The odds don't change - it's still an 18 out of 37 (European wheel) or 38 (American wheel) shot for your winning red on the next spin.

Remember, it's only a wheel. It has no memory, no brain. It doesn't know who you are, what you're betting, or that seven times in a row, black came up on it.

So back to the game. Heaven forbid that two more spins should go against you, for then you'll be faced with the following:

MARTINGALE PROGRESSION CONTINUED

Loss	Initial Bet	Total Loss
8th	$128.00	$255.00
9th	$256.00	$511.00
10th	$512.00	-

Add up these numbers than get out the Pepto-Bismol. Think twice before using this classic system. Do you really want to risk a situation where you'll need to bet over five hundred dollars just to win $1.00?

The Grand Martingale

If you liked the above example, you'll love this system. The rallying point of the **Grand Martingale** is to attempt to win more than $1.00 on a losing progression by adding $1.00 to the bet after each loss. We'll spare ourselves the anguish of adding up these numbers, but you can see they'll add up even faster than the Martingale, and should things go badly, the bets get scary in a real hurry.

The Pyramid System

This system is far more appealing to the player for its winning approach doesn't entail the kind of deep ditch digging that the Martingale and Grand Martingale do.

In this system, also called the **D'Alembert**, we'll look at each bet it terms of units, and to make life easy, we'll use $1.00 as our unit bet. The first bet will be $1.00. If we win, the sequence is ended, and we'll begin a new one.

If the bet is lost, our next bet becomes $2.00. Each subsequent loss adds $1.00 to the bet, so that five consecutive losses would produce a $6.00 bet on the following play. (Compare this to the Martingale, where you'd be watching a $32.00

bet gracing the tables for your $1.00 win, and the first tinges of a headache beginning to pound your skull.)

This system is interesting for after every win, you will decrease your bet by one unit! The end result of this system is that every win (as opposed to every progression) produces a win of $1.00, or if you prefer to think in terms of units, every win produces a one unit gain.

Every won bet is $1.00 more than the previous lost bet.

Let's follow a progression to see how this works.

PYRAMID PROGRESSION

Bet	Result	Total
$1.00	Win	+$1.00
$1.00	Loss	$0.00
$2.00	Loss	-$2.0
$3.00	Win	+$1.00
$2.00	Win	+$3.00
$1.00	Loss	+$2.00
$2.00	Loss	+$0.00
$3.00	Loss	-$3.00
$4.00	Loss	-$7.00
$5.00	Loss	-$12.00
$6.00	Win	-$6.00
$5.00	Loss	-$11.00
$6.00	Win	-$5.00
$5.00	Win	$0.00

TOTAL: 14 Plays: 6 Wins, 8 Losses

You can see the attractions of this system, for despite sustaining five straight losses and eight overall as against only six wins, the sequence where we left off showed the player dead even. A win on the next play would forge a profit of $4.00, with the next bet being $3.00, so the bettor's position looks pretty good overall.

This is all well and good on a short run look.

However, in the long run, this system like all others trying to fight a game where the house has an edge, will ultimately lose. As the progression continues, there will be more losses than wins and the downward dips will be deeper and more frequent than wins.

As long as this is kept in mind, the immovable house edge, than one might play this system to great enjoyment, and in the short run, maybe some profit!

Biased Wheels

There is a way to beat the casino at roulette, but this involves finding an imbalanced wheel, presumably old and rickety, more likely in a smaller casino, or perhaps at a fair where the mechanics of the wheel are far from state of the art.

It is impossible to make a perfectly balanced wheel, one where each number has exactly the same chance of coming up as any other number. A slight imperfection in the material, normal wear and tear, a warp, a tiny tilt, an unlevel floor, a slightly larger or shorter slot - these possibilities or any of a number of others can cause an imbalance of a wheel and favor some numbers to be spun more than others.

Wheels are made with such tremendous precision nowadays that it is extremely unlikely to find a wheel with a bias significant enough to make this theory interesting.

However, you may find an older wheel in use, one that's been subjected to enough wear and tear of normal usage that a bias is created, or one with faulty mechanics, and until the casino has figured out that you've got something going on and shuts down the wheel, you can make a lot of money - with the odds.

First you must determine if the wheel is biased and how large the bias is. To do this requires a lot of work and patience, but if indeed your hunch is right and the wheel is significantly biased, you will have made the effort worthwhile.

To properly track a wheel, you'll need a partner or an associate or two for every spin of the wheel will need to be recorded for at least 24 hours to get a fair sampling. A sampling taken for less than 24 hours will only show short run deviations (unless the wheel is incredibly biased) and may not be an accurate look at biased numbers.

The expectation of any single number being spun is one in 37. For a bias to be effective and show profits, a single number's bias must not only be greater than the 1/37 expected result, but be sufficient enough to overcome the inherent casino's edge of 5.26% on an American wheel and 2.70% on a European one for single zero betting.

You may find one number or several that stand out on a wheel as being biased and base your winning strategy on those numbers (or number). The superior odds inherent in single zero roulette make those games much better to track for if a bias is found, the smaller house edge is easier to overcome and the profits will be greater.

WINNING AT SLOTS

INTRODUCTION

These ever-popular machines can be found around the world, buzzing, clanging and spitting out rewards to their faithful players. Millions are hooked on the game. Some play for the sheer pleasure, hoping to pass a little time and win a few coins, others play for that elusive thing, the big jackpot, which will set them on *easy street*.

In this section we'll show the basics of slots play including the different types of machines available, the percentage returns and payoffs, and of course, some strategy tips for winning big jack-pots!

Let's now take a closer look at the game of slots and the exciting possibilities it holds in store for you.

The History of Slots

Charles Fey is credited with being the originator of slot machines in their more or less current format. His original machines, called **Liberty Bells**, were introduced in the late 1800s and first began to appear in the bars and saloons around the San Francisco Bay. There were coin-operated machines before Fey which were based on games of chance such as dice and roulette, but Fey's Liberty Bell was the first to feature a three reel design with automatic payouts to the winners.

These early machines used three reels of ten symbols each, among which were the famous Liberty Bell figures, along with other symbols of the times such as horseshoes. If the 10 possibilities per reel are multiplied by three reels, 10 x 10 x 10, we come up with 1,000 different possible combinations on these early machines.

Fey set the machines to pay back 86% to the players. The other 14%, the profit, he split 50-50 with the bar and saloon owners. The machines really took off and spurred a host of competitors, most notably Herbert Stephen Mills and the Caille Brothers. Slots have come a long way since then and account for important parts of a casino's income.

Nowadays, names such as Bally and International Game Technology are the big players and the old 5¢ machines, though still to be found, have given way to 25¢, $1.00 and even $100 slots!

THE SLOTS SETTING

Slot machines are grouped together in groups called **banks**. A bank of machines might consist of four machines grouped together in a squarish shape, with backs toward the middle, and fronts facing outward towards the players, or even in larger groups of eight, ten, fifteen, or even more machines, in circular or rectangular shapes.

Often, banks of machines are built around a platform manned by an attractive slots girl whose job is to give the players change when needed, and keep the customers happy and playing. These configurations are called **carousels**.

Within each bank of machines there are a variety of machines. You may see two, three, four or more machines of the same type from the same manufacturer, next to a few from another within the same bank, or even alternating machines with no particular pattern you can discern.

What a group of machines in a bank or carousel will share in common are the coin values. A bank of slots will usually contain machines using the same coin denomination. It is unusual to see different denominations such as 25¢ and $1 machines mixed together within the same bank.

Chairs

Each slot machine in the casino has a chair in front of it, so that you can play the machines in comfort, even if you were to go for hours, which many of the players do.

Plastic Buckets

Throughout the slots area, between the machines, sometimes on top or at the ends of aisles, will be plastic buckets. They look like small ice buckets emblazoned with the name and logo of the casino on them, but it's not cold cubes they're meant to hold. It's coins, bucketfuls of them.

These plastic buckets are widely used by slots players to hold their coins after cashing out from a machine, so that they can transport their haul over to the cashier's cage. You'll often see players scooping coins out of the coin well and shoveling them into their buckets prior to leaving the machine. Some players will use the buckets while they play as well, as a convenient way to hold multiple coins.

THE ELEMENTS OF A SLOT MACHINE

Slot machines are composed of various functioning parts you should be familiar with, and we'll go over them here.

The Reels

The spinning mechanism containing the symbols on a slots machine are the **reels,** technically known as **stepper reels** for the various "steps" or "stops" on the reels. A typical slots machine will contain three reels, much as the earliest machines did back when Fey invented the slot machine, though there are machines with four reels or more in use as well.

Each reel on a slots machine contains a number of **steps** or **stops**, places where the wheel can end when it is spun. This stop may contain a **symbol**, such as a cherry or lemon, or it may even contain a **blank**, a stop with no symbol.

On the new generation of microchip machines, the concept of a stop differs from the electromechanical and earlier predecessors in that the "stop" is no longer necessarily a physical place where the reel stopped, but a *simulated* place. A computer program might simulate a wheel containing 106 blanks to go along with the 22 symbols. The frequency of hits and number of payouts would be set by the program designer, and that total combination of possibilities, as set by the manufacturer, would determine the percentage payout that might be expected by the player.

The Payline

The glass window in front of a slot machine's reels is marked by a horizontal line, called a **payline**. Winning combinations must line up directly behind this line for the spin to be a paying winner. That's why it's called the *payline*. If winning symbols line up, but they're not directly behind the payline, then the spin is not a winner. All winning spins in slots must appear behind the payline.

Some machines have three or five paylines. When there are three paylines, they will generally be lined up as three horizontals, one in the middle, and one each above and below that line. Usually, it takes one coin for each payline to be activated. Machines with five paylines generally add two diagonal paylines. These slots generally need the full five coins for all paylines to be active.

WINNING AT SLOTS

The Payout Display

On the top of each slot machine will be a **payout display** with a colorful attractive design listing all the winning combinations that can be spun and the number of coins or absolute dollar amount that will be paid when there is a winner. Other special winning combinations or conditions will be printed here as well.

The payout display will show the winning payouts for every coin played, and if the machine is a progressive, will either show the progressive total on the machine itself, or be marked "Progressive." When "Progressive" is indicated on the payout display, that progressive jackpot total will be prominently displayed on a large display sign above the bank of progressive machines.

Service Light/Candle Light

On top of each slot machine will be a red indicator light, known as the **Service Light**, or **Candle Light**, which will light up whenever the services of a slots employee is needed. The red light will be activated, that is lit, when the player presses the CHANGE button requesting assistance, when the machine malfunctions, or when a jackpot is hit and the machine is unable to payout the full amount of coins. The last condition is the one we really like to see, that and all the noise that comes with it too.

The Coin Tray

On the bottom facing of each tray is a metal tray, called the **coin tray**. This is where the coins pour out of a machine on winning combinations, or really, on the new machines, only when the CASH OUT button is pushed causing the machine to disgorge it's full bevy of winnings. Bang! Bang! Bang!

The Slots Handle

Pulling on the slots handle, which is a long handle located on the right side of slot machines, will spin the reels, provided of course, that coins are deposited into the machine or credits have been played. Using the handle is the traditional way of spinning the reels and playing slots, and is still preferred by many players. We'll see how long they remain, for play by the credit button is easier and probably the playing style of choice for modern players.

While the result of pulling the slots handle is exactly the same as when it was first created almost 100 years ago, there is a major difference in its actual functionality. Originally, pulling the handle would mechanically set the reels in motion. Now, it does no such thing. Slot machines are microchip units and not mechanically triggered, Pulling the handle on modern machines activates the software which sets the reels in motion, a quantum difference from the pre-80's machines.

THE PLAY BUTTONS

In this section, we describe the active play buttons you might find on a slots machine. Note that some of the buttons listed may have slightly different names, depending upon the manufacturer, but in general, whether called by one name or another, they serve the same function.

Spin Reels

When coins are inserted into the machine, or less than the full amount of credits are played, you will have to manually press the SPIN REELS button to spin the reels and get the action going. (You can also pull the slots handle.)

Play Max Credits/Bet Max Coins

Pressing the PLAY MAX CREDITS button will play the full amount of credits allowed on the machine and automatically spin the reels. Thus, if the machine accepts five coins as a bet, pressing PLAY MAX CREDITS will deduct five coins from your credits. Similarly, if three coins were the maximum bet, then three coins would be played and that amount would be deducted.

This button may also read as BET MAX COINS or PLAY ALL CREDITS, or may have another similar designation which would amount to the same thing. The PLAY MAX CREDITS button will only activate the reels (and deduct the coins played) if money is in the credit. If there is no credit accrued in the machine, you will have to insert more money into the heart of the beast, and play off of that until credits are reestablished.

Play Two Credits, Three Credits

On some machines that accept two coins or three coins, you may see a button that states PLAY TWO COINS or PLAY THREE COINS. These would serve the same function as the PLAY MAX CREDITS button. For example, if you saw PLAY TWO COINS on a machine, that machine would most likely accept two coins as the maximum bet. Pressing the button would deduct two from your credits and spin the reels.

These buttons also may read as BET TWO COINS, PLAY TWO CREDITS, BET THREE COINS, or PLAY THREE CREDITS.

Play One Credit

For players who prefer playing one credit at a time, the slots have a "PLAY ONE CREDIT" button on every machine. Pressing this button will play one credit toward the next pull. Note: this will not automatically activate the reels as the PLAY MAX CREDITS button will do.

However, nothing will happen, that is, the reels will not spin until the handle is pulled or the SPIN REELS button is pressed.

You can also pay two credits by pressing the "Play One Credit" button twice, or three coins by pressing it three times, or the maximum number of credits by pressing this button until the full allowance of coins is reached.

This button may also read as BET ONE COIN or PLAY ONE CREDIT, or have another similar designation amounting to the same thing.

The Cash Out Button

The CASH OUT button, when pressed, converts all the credits built up over the playing session into coins that drop like a metal waterfall into the coin drop below. Players use the CASH OUT button, located prominently on the front of the machine, when they're ready to change machines, to call it a day at the machines altogether, or simply to hear the victory charge of coins pounding into the coin drop. The sound of coins dropping is always fun!

The Change Button

On the far left position on the button display will be a CHANGE button. This convenient button brings you door to door service from the changeperson. (Normally *changegirl*, but males do occupy these formerly all-female jobs in some casinos now.) Pressing the CHANGE button lights up the red candle light at the top of your machine and lets the attendants know that you need service.

THE DISPLAYS

There will be several displays on the front of the machine. While different slots may display the information in different locations, and include things others won't, the basic information will remain the same and be part of any modern slot machine.

Credits Played or Coins Played

The **Credits Played** display shows how many coins are being bet on this particular spin. This display may also be listed as **Coins Played**. Thus, if three coins are played, the display would indicate the number "3" for your information.

Credits

The **Credits** indicator shows how many credits you have accumulated either through winning spins, or through money entered into the machine. Each credit shown will reflect the denomination of coin you're playing.

For example, placing a $20 bill into a 25¢ machine will enter eighty 25¢ credits into your account. The indicator in Credits will read "80." If you play three credits, the Credits will read "77", and if that spin is a win for 20 credits, the Credits will read "97" to reflect the 20 coins win. If that $20 was entered in a dollar machine, then 20 credits "20" would be entered, or "400" on a 5¢ machine.

Playing the PLAY ONE CREDIT or PLAY ALL CREDITS button will automatically deduct those credits from your bankroll.

You can use your credits by either playing them through until the total is down to 0, (which means you've lost them all!), or hitting the CASH OUT button, which will convert credit into actual coins and send them noisily tumbling into the coin well.

Winner Paid

The **Winner Paid** indicator displays the amount won on the current spin. For example, if three liberty bells align for a winning combination paying 40 coins, the Winner Paid display will read "40".

Insert Coin

When the machine is awaiting a play, the **Insert Coin** message will be lit. This lets the player know that he or she will need to drop some action into the machine to initiate play.

THE BASICS OF PLAY

Slots are easy to play. Machines generally take anywhere from 1 to 5 coins, and all one needs to do is insert the coins into the machine, pull the handle and see what Lady Luck brings.

There are many types of slot machine configurations but all work according to the same principles - the paying combinations that are always posted on the machine itself must be lined up in the window for a winner.

Often, the number of lines the machine will pay on depends on the amount of coins deposited. One coin only may pay the middle line, a second coin will pay the top line as well, a third coin - the bottom line, so now any of the three horizontals will pay should a paying combination be hit. A fourth coin may pay the diagonal, and a fifth, the other diagonal.

If the proper combination is hit, the machine should make a little noise for you as coins automatically pour into the well at the bottom. And should a really large payoff be hit, a **jackpot**, the machines will make a bunch of noise, a light may go off atop the machine and you just hang tight, for a casino employee should be there soon to give you the payoff.

More winning rows played does not necessarily equate to better odds of winning. The odds are built into the machine and no amount of lines played will change them.

The most important factor affecting your chances at winning and the percentages at which you're gambling is how loose or tight the machines are set by the casino - that is what determines the odds facing a slots player.

WINNING CASINO PLAY

Object of the Game

The goal in slots is to get the symbols on the reels to line up directly behind the payline, in one of the winning combinations listed on the front of the machine. The higher ranked the combination, as listed, the greater the payout will be.

For some players, the real goal in slots is to hit the jackpot paying thousands of dollars, tens of thousand of dollars, or even millions of dollars on the big progressives. The particular goal at a machine, at least the big goal, is a function of the machine itself. Machines have a variety of jackpot sizes and rewards, but whatever the machine, you'd like to hit the big one.

All right, let's face it. The real goal for many of you is to hit paydirt, one pull, and it's off to Hawaii for a year or more as the first stop on your post-retirement trans-world luxury cruise. Plush bathrobes, and all that, the ability to do whatever you want, whenever you want, without answering to the bossman anymore. Not a bad goal.

Coin Denominations

Slot machines come in a variety of coin denominations, enough choice to meet any player's need. You can play the **small coin** machines, 5¢,

WINNING AT SLOTS

10¢, and 25¢, the **medium coin** machines, 50¢ or
$1, or the **big coin** machines, $5, $25, $100, and
$500 slots! You saw it right. There are $500 coin
babies out there and they do get action.

The most popular machines played are the 25¢
and $1 machines, though where available, the 5¢
slots get good action sometimes as well. The big
coin machines are sparingly found only in the larger
casinos, while the 10¢ and 50¢ machines, are not as
readily found.

Playing by Coin

Most players get going on the slot machines in
the time-honored way of dropping coins directly
into the machine, a method that hasn't changed
from the original pre-slots designs more than a
hundred years ago.

Playing by Credits

Depositing coins into the machine is not the
only way to play the slots; you can also play on
credits. Once you have credits, spinning the reels at
slots is as easy as easy could be. On every machine,
you'll see a button marked "PLAY MAX COINS,"
"PLAY THREE COINS," "PLAY FIVE CRED-
ITS," or similar buttons indicating that you can use

the credits for play. This button will typically be found on the right side of the machine near the coin acceptor, the area of the machine most convenient for easy play. You can expect this button to be large and easily visible.

Pressing this button automatically spins the reels if you have credits available. Experienced slots players use this button as if it were a speed dial. Press, result, press result, press result. They'll run through spins so fast, they'll cycle through three or even five spins in as quick a time as a player using coins gets off one spin of the reels. Serious slots players love the credit button for its ease of play and speed. You'll find it a great feature too.

If no credits are available, pressing this button won't activate anything if you have no credits to play on. To get things going again, you'll need to deposit more coins into the coin slot, or slide another bill into the hungry machine.

The Slots Handle

The traditional way of playing the slots is to use the handle located at the side of the machine to spin the reels.

Slot machines today are caught between the new and the old. The reels can be activated by either pulling the handle, or pressing a button on the machine. Casinos prefer that players use the faster method of playing by button (and by credits), since it generates more dollars played per hour and higher profits. With both slots handle and button at their disposal, the style of play used is totally at the players discretion.

Experienced slots players tend to use the button more than the handle. They want the fast action and easy play of the buttons, especially since they camp out at their machines for hours at a time. Tourists and casual players, on the other hand, lean more towards the handle pull. These players are in no rush and like the full enjoyment of the physical participation. Slots, to many beginning players, usually means pulling the handle.

Establishing Credits

There are two ways to establish credits at a machine. The basic way of building credits is by simply putting coins in the machine. Once coins are in, you can play. Now, with the new bill acceptors inserted into the latest versions of machines, you can immediately establish credits by inserting a $20 or $100, for example, into the machine. These credits will register on the display of the machine marked "Credits."

The second way, which is relatively new to slots play, is to earn these credits through wins. After every win, the amount won automatically gets credited to your total. This amount will be posted underneath the area marked "credits " on the machine.

For example, if you line up a combination that pays 18 coins, the number "18" will be posted for your credits. If you already had 50 credits accrued, then the win of 18 would be added to that total for a new total of "68."

You can play on these credits as long as you have them, or cash out at any time by pressing the "CASH OUT" button.

SLOTS TIP

Never, ever leave a machine that owes you money. Wait for the attendants to come by no matter how long it takes. You should as soon leave your wallet on a New York city street corner as walk away from a machine that's stacked with winning credits.

TYPES OF MACHINES

In this section, we'll look at the various type of slot machines available for play, from the older style single coin machines, to the multi-coin machines, multipliers, progressives, Big Berthas, Buy-Your-Play, and Wild Symbol machines.

Single Coin Machines

The single coin machines, soon to be a dying breed, used to be the only type of slots available to the player, that is, until the invention of the multiple coin type machine. Now single coin machines are rarely found, being much less profitable for the casino than a machine which takes two, three, or even five times as many coins, and by the same token, being that much less exciting to the players.

Multipliers

A multiplier is a slot machine that accepts multiple coins (as opposed to a single coin) for play, and pays winning combinations proportionately higher for each coin played except typically, for the biggest jackpot payoff, where a win for the maximum number of coins played is much larger than if just one or two coins were deposited. This is how casinos encourage players to bet the max on all plays.

The typical multipliers accept either two, three or five coins as the standard maximum play. When two coins are played for example, a winning spin will pay double a single coin for the same winning combination, three coins will pay three times, and five coins will pay five times. For example, if hitting three cherries pays two coins when a single coin is bet, three coins would yield a payout of six coins.

Soon, there will be machines that accept much larger numbers of coins for a single play - that is simply inevitable.

Multiple Payline Machines

Much like bingo, the multiple payline machines give slots players multiple directions that can turn into a winner. The single payline machine has one line across the machine, which shows where the reels must line up for a winning combination to be paid. The multiple payline machine, on the other hand, has three or five lines, depending upon the machine, which gives players more winning positions on the reels.

On these machines, each coin inserted activates another payline. On a three payout line machine, there will be three horizontal lines. One line will go right across the middle as in a single payout line machine, a second line will be above, and the third line will be below. To the left of each line, on the display, will be marked something like 1st coin payline for the center line, 2nd coin payline for the top line, and 3rd coin payline for the lower line. As each coin is inserted, the payline boxes will light up indicating that they're in play.

The five coin payline machines have two additional lines that crisscross the payout area diagonally. Appropriately, these machines are referred to as five line criss-cross machines, or simply criss-cross machines. These machines will have additional boxes indicating 4th coin payline and 5th coin payline. These two indicators will light up when the fourth and fifth coins are inserted.

Winning spins can now be formed in any of the five directions on the five line machine, or on the three horizontals on the three line machine.

Keep in mind that while there may be more ways to win with these new directions and lines, the overall chances of you winning are no better or worse than any other slots machine. These odds are set by the casinos on a machine by machine basis. If the payback percentages are set higher, you'll have a better chance of winning, and if they are set lower, than your chances are worse.

Buy-Your-Pay Machines

The buy-your-pay slots work on a different concept than the other machines you'll find. These machines have a single payout line and typically accept up to three or five coins. They will only pay on certain symbols if enough coins are played. For example, the first coin might only credit cherries as the winner, but if another winner is hit, such as the bars, or sevens, it won't pay because the requisite number of coins weren't inserted!

These machines are less prevalent now than before, but since they can still be found, you'll need to be on guard if you find yourself playing them. Again, if playing buy-your-pay machines, always play the maximum number of coins.

Wild Play Machines

The latest craze in slot machines are the wild play machines. These fun machines give players a chance to double, triple or even quintuple (five times) their winning payout if a wild symbol lines up as part of their winning combination. And if two wild symbols line up as part of that combination, the winning payout will be multiplied by four times, nine times and twenty-five times respectively.

When three wild symbols show, they are their own winning combination, and are not multiplied by each other as with two wild symbols. You'll see that condition listed on the front of the slots.

These new machines add a lot to the excitement to the game, especially when they are hit. It's always fun to watch a winning combination take off when a wild symbol or even two is hit.

IGT is leading the way with their very popular Double and Triple Diamond machines. The wild symbol on these machines is of course, the diamond. These machines are the most wildly sold slot machines in the industry, and the most popular. You also might see machines on the floor with a five times multiplier. New machines are being developed and marketed all the time so you'll have to keep your eyes open for other exciting concepts as well.

Progressives

Progressives feature a growing jackpot which increases each time a coin is inserted into a machine that is hooked up to the progressive. When the jackpot does hit, the lucky player wins the total accumulated in the jackpot. At the same time, the jackpot total will be reset to a predetermined total, ready to begin climbing again.

Progressive jackpots can be relatively high if they've gone a while without hitting, or low if they have been hit recently.

Following are two special types of progressive machines.

Mega Progressive Machines

The progressive slot machines draw tremendous amounts of excitement among players. The dream of hitting a one million dollar jackpot with one pull of the handle gets players excited. However, a one million dollar jackpot is a "small" jackpot nowadays. As more players get into these linked progressives, the jackpots are now in the millions. Five million dollar jackpots, ten million dollar jackpots, and even bigger ones are being hit by lucky players now.

Megabucks, and Quartermania, are two inter-casino linked mega-progressives with enormous jackpots.

Multiple Progressives

A newer type of machine has appeared on the slots scene, and that is the multiple progressives. For example, the Cool Millions slots by CDS Gaming, a one payline machine, offers players a chance to win three types of progressives. The big progressive, which on the machine I saw was $500,067.95, is won by lining up the three cool million symbols on the payline. The next two progressives, in the three thousand range but of varying amounts, were won by lining up three sevens, one set of either red or blue. There were other payouts as well.

Big Berthas

The classic Big Bertha machines are gigantic slot machines of many reels, usually eight to ten, that are strategically placed by casinos near their front entrance (usually, but not always) to lure curious players into their casinos for a pull or two. These novelty machines are always a fun distraction for passerby's new to casinos, and gives them one more wow on top of all the other wows confronting them in these strange casino environments.

While the payout percentage on Big Berthas isn't very high, and the machines are mostly played by tourists for a pull or two, it is enjoyable for first-timers to pull the handle on the largest slot machine breed in the world.

SLOTS CLUBS

The greatest boon to hit slots players yet, the slots clubs, are the best way for slots players to amass a seemingly endless parade of room comps, meal comps, show comps, line passes, and even cash rebates. In fact, if you play your "reels" right, you can virtually enjoy free vacations doing just what you like to do best in the casinos - playing the slots! And that's not bad at all.

Slots players are no longer taken for granted. With slots revenues in the billions worldwide, that's right, billions, casinos are realizing who their important players really are, and are actively pursuing their patronage. Comps, incentives, and bonuses, once reserved for table players, are now in the full domain of the slots player.

That's great news for slots players because casinos are motivated to get you to their machines as opposed to their competitors machines, a situation we'll show you how to take advantage of to your full benefit.

Slots clubs are basically enrollment programs that players sign up for as members. There is no charge to become a member, but lots of benefits. The concept is simple. Once enrolled as a member, the casinos will issue a member card with the players name and card number. These cards get inserted into the machines prior to play and automatically track the players betting action. The more action a player gives the casino, the greater the benefits he enjoys just for playing the machines. And what could be better?

For example, in some casinos, players can accrue enough credits after approximately just one hour of action at the $1 machines, or 2-3 hours at the 25¢ machines, that they can qualify for benefits. Benefits and comps are all a function of the amount of money played. For example if you're playing $1 slots, three coins at a time, and play 500 spins, you've given the casino $1,500 worth of action, 500 spins by $3 each. If you're playing quarters, five at a time to a machine, and play 1,000 spins, your action is equal to 5,000 quarters, or $1,250.

Note that the action given to a machine or a casino is not measured by how much you've won or lost, but the total amount of plays multiplied by the amount bet.

And that's why slots clubs are so great. If you're going to be playing the machines anyway, you're guaranteed "winnings," so to speak, by dint of the simple fact that your action is earning rewards.

Each casino has their own slots program, some with greater benefits than others. But all are worth joining if you plan to play slots at a casino, and especially if you plan on playing a lot of slots.

If you're going to be playing the slots, you should definitely join a slots club. There is no membership price or costs of any type to be a member. Outside of the few minutes it might take to do the application process that gets you going - which is nothing more than getting your basic information - the membership has nothing to do with income level or credit information - there is no other effort needed to enjoy the many benefits.

Joining a slots club is as easy as filling an application form. The Slots Hosts are usually located in the rear of the casinos, but if you can't find them, ask any of the personnel and they can probably send you in the right direction. I usually find that the security guards are the best to ask, especially in the casinos that have a security officer posted at a central desk near the cashier's cage.

Your first move, upon approaching a machine and readying yourself for play, is to insert your card into the card reader. Upon insertion, the card will usually identify you by name, though sometimes, the casino may have a theme greeting instead. Every slot machine in the casino has a card reader that will accept your club card for play. These are typically found in the front of the machines, though they may be on the sides.

If for some reason you can't find the reader, or have trouble inserting your card into it, or have any other problem, call over one of the slots personnel. They'll be glad to help you get set up.

SAMPLE SLOTS PAYOFF
(per one coin)

Winning Combination	Payoff
7-7-7	100 coins
Bar-Bar-Bar	50 coins
Bell-Bell-Bell	20 coins
Bell-Bell-Bar	18 coins
Bar-Bell-Bell	18 coins
Plum-Plum-Plum	20 coins
Plum-Plum-Bar	14 coins
Bar-Plum-Plum	14 coins
Orange-Orange-Orange	20 coins
Orange-Orange-Bar	10 coins
Bar-Orange-Orange	10 coins
Cherry-Cherry-Cherry	20 coins
Any-Cherry-Cherry	5 coins
Cherry-Cherry-Any	5 coins
Cherry-Any-Cherry	5 coins
Any-Any-Cherry	2 coins
Cherry-Any-Any	2 coins

SLOT PERCENTAGES

The percentage return of slot machines vary from casino to casino, and often within a casino as well. While the Nevada regulatory commission sets no minimum at all, the Atlantic City gaming commission requires a minimum return of 83% back to the players. Within these loose frameworks, a whole range of percentages may apply.

In general, a casino that relies on slots for a good portion of their income will offer players a higher return on their slots money, while those that have the slots as but an incidental income, will pay less on the average.

Some casinos advertise slots with returns as high as 97% to the player, others, even as high as 99%! Obviously, the player stands a much better chance of winning at these places than others where a standard return of only 83% might be the norm. On machines in areas not covered by regulatory minimums, such as Nevada, players may not even get an 83% return.

WINNING STRATEGIES

Players are always asking me, "Are there really winning strategies at slots? After all, all you do is pull the handle and either win or lose, isn't that right?" My answer to them, is that it isn't correct, no more so than craps is all luck because all you do is throw the dice. There *are* better ways to play, methods that increase your chances of winning.

There are ways to maximize your chances of

winning in the short term by playing the proper amount of coins, strategies to increase your chances of the big jackpot, strategies to take advantage of the benefits casinos give to slots players, better casinos to play in and better machines to choose from, and finally, ways to maximize winnings and minimize losing through money management strategies. Knowing how to properly play the slots can make the difference between winning and losing.

We'll cover a few basic concepts here, but I would refer the reader to my book, the *Secrets of Winning Slots* for a full treatment of the 20 winning strategies at slots.

The most important concept in slots is to locate the machines with the loosest setting, or with progressive machines, to play only the machines with the highest progressive setting.

The first thing to look for are casinos which really push their slot machine business and cater to the players, and also casinos which advertise a higher return. These are places that may offer slot players a better than average return.

In general, the poorer paying machines will be located in areas where the casino or proprietor hopes to grab a few of the bettor's coins as he passes through an area or waits on a line. Airport terminals, restaurant and show lines, bathrooms and the like tend to have smaller returns.

On the other hand, casinos that specialize in slots and look to attract serious players, will set up slots areas within a casino that will have better payoffs, or even, as you can find in Las Vegas, the whole casino will be slots only! These casinos view slots as an important income, and in order to keep regular slots customers, their players must hear those jackpot bells ringing - after all, winning is contagious!

Some machines are set to pay better than others, and these slots will be mixed in with poorer paying ones, so its always a good idea to look for the hot machine. Better yet, ask the change girls. They spend all day near the slots and know which machines tend to return the most money.

Basically, your best strategy is to examine the wide array of machines offered for play, and to find the best one suited to your personal style.

When you hit a good jackpot, make sure you set your stop-loss limit. This guarantees that you walk away a winner!

WINNING
AT
VIDEO POKER

INTRODUCTION

Video poker is a lot of fun, for decision-making and skill are involved and even better, proper play can bring you profits! The game can be as leisurely or hurried as you want for there is no dealer to hurry you along. You choose your own pace - it's just you against the machine. May the best one win!

The whole setting is really simple. All one needs is some coins to play and an available video poker machine, and you're in business.

This section shows you the basic rules of play, how to work the video poker machines, the different machines available, the payoffs and winning hands, and most importantly, a winning strategy to arm you with the best odds and make you a winner.

PLAYER ADVANTAGE IN VIDEO POKER!

There is a big reason for video poker's increasing popularity - with proper play you can actually have the edge over the casino, and like blackjack, have the expectation of winning money every time you play!

That's right, with proper strategy, you'll have the edge in video poker and if that isn't incentive to put a little study in the game and improve your odds, I'm not sure what is.

What we'll show you in this section is a simplified basic strategy that will improve your odds and get your game going in the right direction.

However, for those players serious about beating the house, you'll want to buy the advanced video poker strategy listed in the back. It takes you beyond the simplified basic strategy presented here and shows you the full Basic Strategy Charts, the advanced strategies, which machines to play for best results and overall, how to be a winner and play video poker for a profit.

THE TYPES OF MACHINES

Video poker offers the player a variety of machines from which to choose. The two basic types of video poker machines are the **Flat-Top** (or **Straight**) machines and the **Progressives**. The Flat-Tops offer set payoffs on all the hands won, with the payoffs proportionately larger for greater amounts of coins played. Thus, a winning payoff on two coins played will be exactly double that for the same winning hand with one coin played.

The one exception is for the royal flush, where a winning payoff will give the player a 4,000 coin return when five coins are played, as opposed to only 200, 400, 600 and 800 coins on a one, two, three and four coin play respectively. All other payoffs are in proportion.

Winning payoffs are posted on the machine, so you can see right off what you're up against.

The Progressive machines differ from the Straight or Flat Tops in that when a royal flush is hit with five coins played, the payoff is not a set amount but is based on a progressive total. This jackpot constantly increases until the royal is hit, when it will start again at a set amount, such as $1,000 on a 25¢ machine.

The Progressives can be exciting for jackpots go higher and higher, and now and again, a quarter machine will soar well into the $2,000+ range or even higher. However, like the Straight machines, the full five coins must be played to reap the full reward when the royal flush is hit.

There are different varieties of the video poker machines within the above classifications.

A player may find Jacks or Better, 10s or Better, Deuces Wild and Joker Wild, and these can be played as Straights or Progressives, depending upon what casino players find themselves in and what machines are offered.

We'll talk more about this later when we discuss each game individually.

HOW TO PLAY

Video poker is basically played as draw poker. The machine uses a 52 card deck which is played fresh after each hand. While you won't receive the same card within a play, for the machine will deal cards from the 52 card computer pack, the memory ends there as the deck is "reshuffled" after each deal.

To start, you need to insert anywhere from one to five coins into the machine. The choice is yours - play one or play five at your discretion. We will recommend that serious players insert the full five coins to get the best odds, but we'll go into that later.

If five coins are inserted, the machine will automatically deal a hand to you. However, if less than the maximum amount is inserted, you'll need to press the button marked **DRAW/DEAL** to receive your cards.

Five cards will show on the screen. These are your cards. You may keep one, some, all or none of the cards. It's your decision. To keep a card, press the button marked "**HOLD**" underneath the corresponding card you wish to keep. There will be five hold buttons, one for each card, and for each card you want to keep, you must press the hold button.

"**HELD**" will appear on the screen underneath each card or cards so chosen. The other cards, the ones you wish to discard, will not be kept by the machine.

What happens if you press the wrong hold button by accident or change your mind? No problem. Press the corresponding button again. If the card indicated "HELD," it will no longer do so and will not be held by the computer. If you change your mind press the button one more time, and again the "HELD" sign will come on the screen indicating that the card will be kept on the draw.

Until you press the draw button, it is not too late to change your strategy decision.

A player may keep all five original cards and does so by pushing the hold button under each card or he or she may discard all five original cards if so desired. This is done by pressing the DRAW/DEAL button without having pressed any of the hold buttons.

You now press the DRAW/DEAL button to receive some new cards. The "HELD" cards will remain and those cards not chosen to be held will be replaced with new ones. This set of cards is the final hand.

If your hand is a winner, the machine will flash "**WINNER**" at the bottom of the screen. Winning hands are automatically paid according to the payoffs shown on the machine.

Credit

There is a useful feature offered on all video poker machines that allows you to play on winnings using a credit function built-in to the machines.

Let's say, for example, that you've just hit a win for 20 coins. Two things will happen.

On the machine, you'll see "Credit - 20" appear. To continue playing without cashing out and reinserting coins, you can now press another button that will have lit up and be indicated by the label, **Maximum Bet**, **Bet 5** or some similar name. This allows you to play five of your 20 credits toward a new hand which will appear on the screen along with the information that your credit now stands at 15.

The second thing that will happen after your 20 coin win is that a button called the **Cashout** or **Payout** button will light up. If pressed, the machine will give immediate payment of the winnings registered in the credit area.

The Cashout button can be used after any hand is completed to cash out wins that have accumulated. If you want to continue playing on credit, keep pressing the Maximum Bet button to get a new hand dealt.

Let's go over the winning hands in video poker and then we'll show the payoffs you'll most likely encounter in the different games available.

WINNING AT VIDEO POKER

The hands in the chart below are listed in ascending order, from weakest to strongest, as they are in the payoff charts in this section, with the exception of the Five of a Kind hand, which is usually stronger than a Royal Flush composed of wild cards but weaker than the Royal made naturally - without wild cards.

WINNING VIDEO POKER HANDS

Jacks or Better - Two cards of equal value are called a pair. Jacks or better refers to a pair of Jacks, Queens, Kings or Aces.

Two Pair - Two sets of paired cards, such as 3-3 and 10-10.

Three of a Kind - Three cards of equal value, such as 9-9-9.

Straight - Five cards in numerical sequence, such as 3-4-5-6-7 or 10-J-Q-K-A. The ace can be counted as the highest card or the lowest card in a straight, however, it may not be in the middle of a five card run, such as Q-K-A-2-3, which is not a straight.

Flush - Any five cards of the same suit, such as five hearts.

Full House - Three of a kind and a pair, such as 2-2-2-J-J.

Four of a Kind - Four cards of equal value, as K-K-K-K.

Straight Flush - A straight all in the same suit, such as 7-8-9-10-J, all in spades.

Royal Flush - 10-J-Q-K-A, all in the same suit.

Five of a Kind - Five cards of equal value, a hand that's only possible in wild card video poker. For example, if deuces are wild, the hand 2-2-7-7-7 would be five sevens.

Jacks or Better: 9-6 Machines

These machines are known as **9-6 machines**, because of the 9 and 6 coin payouts when the Full House and Flush are hit. Note that a pair of 10s will not pay anything back, nor will any lower pair. A hand of jacks or better is needed for a payout.

PAYOFFS ON JACKS OR BETTER 9-6 MACHINE

Coins Played	1	2	3	4	5
Jacks or Better	1	2	3	4	5
Two Pair	2	4	6	8	10
Three of a Kind	3	6	9	12	15
Straight	4	8	12	16	20
Flush	6	12	18	24	30
Full House	9	18	27	36	45
Four of a Kind	25	50	75	100	125
Straight Flush	50	100	150	200	250
Royal Flush	250	500	750	1000	4000

Progressive Payout

Besides the straight machines discussed above, there are Progressive machines, as in slots.

All payoffs, like the straight machines are fixed except in the case of a Royal Flush, where this grandaddy pays the accumulated total posted above the machine on the electronic board. This total slowly, but constantly rises, and on a quarter machine in Las Vegas can rise into the thousands of dollars.

The following chart shows typical payoffs for video poker on a Jacks or Better Progressive machine. This machine is known as an **8-5 machine**, so named for the payoffs given on the full house and flush respectively.

PAYOFFS ON JACKS OR BETTER 8-5 PROGRESSIVES				
Coins Played 1	2	3	4	5
Jacks or Better 1	2	3	4	5
Two Pair 2	4	6	8	10
Three of a Kind 3	6	9	12	15
Straight 4	8	12	16	20
Flush 5	10	15	20	25
Full House 8	16	24	32	40
Four of a Kind 25	50	75	100	125
Straight Flush 50	100	150	200	250
Royal Flush 250	500	750	1000	*

*When five coins are played and the royal flush is hit, the bettor receives the full amount accumulated for the Progressive jackpot. Note that all five coins must be played to win the jackpot.

10s or Better Video Poker

The 10s or Better machine is only found infrequently. The following is the payout on the non-progressive machines. Note that Royal Flushes pay 800-1 only if five coins have been played.

PAYOFFS ON 10S OR BETTER

Coins Played	1	2	3	4	5
10s or Better	1	2	3	4	5
Two Pair	2	4	6	8	10
Three of a Kind	3	6	9	12	15
Straight	4	8	12	16	20
Flush	5	10	15	20	25
Full House	6	12	18	24	30
Four of a Kind	25	50	75	100	125
Straight Flush	50	100	150	200	250
Royal Flush	250	500	750	1000	4000

Wild Card Video Poker

Two variations of video poker that have caught on and gained in popularity are the **Deuces Wild** and **Jokers Wild** machines. Wild cards can be given any value or suit and the machine will interpret wild cards in the most advantageous way for the player.

For example, the hand 2 2 5 6 8 in Deuces Wild would be a straight, for one 2 can be used as a 7 and the other as either a 9 or 4. The deuces could also be used as eights to give three of a kind, but since the straight is more valuable to the player the machine will see it as a straight.

Wild card machines have different payoff schedules than the Jacks or Better machines, and these machines will start giving credit only on a three of a kind hand or better.

Deuces Wild Video Poker

This variation of video poker is played the same way as the Jacks or Better or 10s or Better machines and uses the same standard 52 card deck, but in this version there is one important difference - the four deuces (2s) are wild, and can be used as any card in the deck, even to make a five of a kind hand.

The video poker machine will recognize the best hand possible using the deuces and will automatically give credit for the maximum hand value that can be made.

DEUCES WILD VIDEO POKER PAYOUT					
Coins Played	**1**	**2**	**3**	**4**	**5**
Three of a Kind	1	2	3	4	5
Straight	2	4	6	8	10
Flush	2	4	6	8	10
Full House	3	6	9	12	15
Four of a Kind	5	10	15	20	25
Straight Flush	9	18	27	36	45
Five of a Kind	15	30	45	60	75
Royal Flush (deuces)	25	50	75	100	125
Four Deuces	200	400	600	800	1000
Royal Flush (Natural)	250	500	750	1000	4000

Note that the Royal Flush as a natural hand (without the deuces) will be paid off at 800-1 only if five coins are played.

Joker Wild Video Poker

There are two version of the Joker Wild game: **Ace-King** and **Two Pairs**. In the Ace-King version, a minimum hand of a pair of kings must be made for a payoff. In Two Pairs, two pair is the minimum hand needed for a payoff.

Both versions of Joker Wild are played with a 53 card deck, the regular 52 card deck plus the wild card, the **joker**, which can be assigned any value.

We'll look at the payoffs for each Joker Wild game. Note that the Royal will only be paid off with the maximum return if five coins are played.

JOKER WILD VIDEO POKER PAYOUT ACE-KING

Coins Played	1	2	3	4	5
Ace or Kings	1	2	3	4	5
Two Pair	1	2	3	4	5
Three of a Kind	2	4	6	8	10
Straight	3	6	9	12	15
Flush	5	10	15	20	25
Full House	7	14	21	28	35
Four of a Kind	20	40	60	80	100
Straight Flush	50	100	150	200	250
Royal Flush (Joker)	100	200	300	400	500
Five of a Kind	200	400	600	800	1000
Royal Flush (natural)	250	500	750	1000	4000

Note the same payout whether one gets a pair of Aces or Kings, or Two Pair.

Sometimes a machine will be found that pays off only 15 for 1 on the four of a kind instead of the 20 for 1 as listed above. Give these machines a miss.

JOKER WILD VIDEO POKER PAYOUT
TWO PAIR

Coins Played	1	2	3	4	5
Two Pair	1	2	3	4	5
Three of a Kind	2	4	6	8	10
Straight	5	10	15	20	25
Flush	7	14	21	28	35
Full House	8	16	24	32	40
Four of a Kind	20	40	60	80	100
Straight Flush	50	100	150	200	250
Royal Flush (Joker)	50	100	150	200	250
Five of a Kind	100	200	300	400	500
Royal Flush (natural)	250	500	750	1000	4000

Note that five coins must be played, and should always be played, to receive the maximum payout for the Royal Flush. For example, the Royal Flush will pay out 4,000 coins or $1,000, for a quarter machine when five coins are played, while four coins would yield only 1/4 as much - $250.

Getting a Straight Flush with five coins will pay 250 coins or $62.50 and a Full House will pay 45 coins or $11.25 for that same quarter machine.

WINNING STRATEGIES

The big payoff on video poker machines is for the royal flush. It doesn't matter what variation is played - Jacks or Better, 10s or Better, Deuces Wild or Joker Wild - a whopping 4,000 coins are paid for this big daddy when five coins are played.

And on progressive machines, if a full five coins are played, the total could be a great deal higher, making the game even more interesting for the player trying to land himself or herself a jackpot to remember.

Of course, the royal doesn't come often. With correct strategy, you'll hit one every 30,000+ hands on the average. This doesn't mean, however, that you won't hit one in your very first hour of play!

But meanwhile, you'll be collecting other winners such as straights, full houses and the like, and with proper play, all in all, you can beat the video poker machines. To win, you must play the correct strategies. Like regular poker, there are skillful ways to play your hand.

However, unlike regular poker, you're not playing against other players, but against a machine, and the strategies must be adjusted accordingly. Strategies that make sense in the Friday night game may not be the proper ones at a video poker machine.

Always Play Five Coins

To achieve the absolute best odds at the video poker machine, five coins must be played. At first glance, this suggestion probably strikes you as being strange. Why not one coin or two? After all, the payoffs on all hands at the video poker machine are proportionately the same whether one, two, three, four or five coins are played.

However, there's one glaring exception - the royal flush.

And though this hand doesn't come often, it does come and much more so than in a regular poker game for we're playing an entirely different strategy in video poker. We're concentrating on the big score, the royal flush, as opposed to a regular poker game, where your primary goal is simply to win the hand, even if a pair of sevens do the trick. And in video poker, a pair of sevens is worth nothing - the machine gives no payoff for it.

We're playing the odds at the machines, and you'll find yourself throwing away hands that you would never do in a regular poker game. But like we mentioned above, video poker is not a regular poker game.

Look back at the payoff chart for Jacks or Better and notice what happens on the royal flush payoffs.

Interesting, yes? One coin played returns 200 coins, two coins yields 400, three coins 600 and four coins brings home 800 bad boys. Well, the progression for the fifth coin should be 1,000 if you're following along with the addition. But it's not.

The full payoff on a royal flush with five coins played is 4,000 coins! Now that's a nice payoff and that's also the reason we're going to be playing five coins. The royal is not as remote as it seems. You may never see one in a regular poker game, but at the video poker machines, following the strategies we suggest, you have a good chance to stare one in the face as the ringing bells mesmerize your gambling psyche.

You'll see similar jumps for the Royal Flush payoffs on all the video poker machines.

Therefore, to collect the full payoff on a royal flush, proper play dictates that you always play the full five coins for each game. For if you do hit the royal flush, there's a big, big difference between 1,000 coins returned and 4,000 returned.

Of course, less serious players can play any amount of coins from 1 to 5 and still enjoy the game.

Find Machines With the Best Payoffs

The payoff schedules we've listed in this section are not the only ones you'll find for the games we've discussed.

You may find machines with less generous payouts, so as a general rule, and when possible, always choose machines with better payouts.

For example, when there's a lot of casino competition, such as Las Vegas, a little window shopping will definitely be to your advantage.

WINNING AT VIDEO POKER

Winning Strategy for Jacks or Better:

Following is the basic strategy for the 9-6 machines. (These strategies are not applicable to the 8-5 Jacks or Better Progressives.)*

1. Whenever you hold <u>four cards to a royal flush,</u> discard the fifth card, even if that card gives you a flush or pair.

2. Keep a <u>jacks or better pair</u> and any higher hand such as a three of a kind or straight over three to the royal. Play the <u>three to a royal</u> over any lesser hand such as a low pair or four flush.

3. With <u>two cards to a royal</u>, keep four straights, four flushes, and high pairs or better instead.

Otherwise, go for the royal.

4. Never break up a <u>straight or flush</u>, unless a one card draw gives you a chance for the royal.

---

*The full strategy charts for the 9-6 machines and the strategy charts for the 8-5 Progressives are beyond the scope of this book. Serious players looking to have the mathematical advantage and win money at video poker must buy GRI's Professional Video Poker Strategy listed in the back.

5. Keep <u>jacks or better</u> over a four straight or four flush.

6. Never break up a <u>four of a kind</u>, <u>full house</u>, <u>three of a kind</u> and <u>two pair</u> hands. The *rags*, worthless cards for the latter two hands, should be dropped on the draw.

7. The <u>jacks or better pair</u> is always kept, except when you have four cards to the royal, or four to the straight flush.

8. Keep <u>low pairs</u> over the four straight, but discard them in favor of the four flushes and three or four to a royal flush.

9. When dealt <u>unmade hands</u>, a pre-draw hands with no payable combination of cards, save in order, four to a royal flush and straight flush, three to a royal flush, four flushes, four straights, three to a straight flush, two cards to the royal, two cards jack or higher and one card jack or higher.

10. Lacking any of the above, with no card jack or higher, discard all the cards and draw five fresh ones.

Simplified Basic Strategy Chart

The following chart sums up the simplified basic strategy for Jacks or Better. The hands are listed in order of strength from most powerful first, the Royal Flush, to the least powerful last, the garbage hands.

Keep the hands listed higher in preference to hands listed lower. For example, you'll keep a High Pair over a three to a royal, but throw it away in favor of a four to the royal.

JACKS OR BETTER
SIMPLIFIED BASIC STRATEGY CHART

Hand to Be Held	Cards Held	Cards Drawn
Royal Flush	5	0
Straight Flush	5	0
Four of a Kind	5	0
Full House	5	0
Four to a Royal	4	1
Flush	5	0
Three of a Kind	3	2
Straight	5	0
Four to a Straight Flush	4	1
Two Pair	4	1
High Pair	2	3
Three to a Royal	3	2
Four to a Flush	4	1
Low Pair	2	3
Four to a Straight	4	1
Three to a Straight Flush	3	2
Two to a Royal	2	3
Two High Cards	2	3
One High Card	1	4
Garbage Hand - Draw Five	0	5

Winning Strategy for 10s or Better

10s or Better is played similarly to Jacks or Better, except that you should keep a pair of 10s instead of discarding them for they yield a pay-off.

Otherwise, follow the strategy as outlined above in Jacks or Better Winning Strategy.

Winning Strategy for Deuces Wild

Deuces are extremely valuable cards so when you get them, make sure you never discard them by accident. You'll notice that there is no payoff for hands less than three of a kind, so our strategy must be adjusted accordingly.

The key in Deuces Wild as in the non-wild versions is to go for the big payouts - the royal flush. Therefore, when you have three cards to-ward a royal flush discard the other two and go for it. Of course, the same holds true when you have four to the royal. Thus, if you have two deuces and a 10 or higher, along with two sub-10 cards of no value, go for the royal.

Similarly, if you have two deuces and three cards below the 10 in value, dump the crap and hang onto the deuces, unless two of the cards are paired in which case you have four of a kind, or the two cards retained give you four cards toward a straight flush.

If you hold one or two deuces with nothing else that's interesting, dump the junk and hang onto the deuces. If you're hand is really poor, and you're dealt five unrelated cards, get rid of them all and go for five fresh ones.

Three card flushes or straights are worthless in this game as are single unmatched high cards so don't be holding onto hands of this nature. You'll also get rid of two pair hands - for they don't pay. Hang onto one of the pairs, and go for three new cards.

If one of the pairs is teamed with a wild deuce, keep the three of a kind. However, if the deuce forms a high pair, it does no good at all and as suggested above, keep the deuce and draw four new cards.

Keep a pair at the outset, unless you've got a three card straight flush or royal flush going, in which case you'll dump the pair and go for the gold.

You'll find that many of the hands you'll be dealt will contain nothing worth saving and you'll be drawing for five fresh cards. Three card straights and flushes fit in this category along with some of the others we've mentioned. In any case, don't be afraid to discard your original five cards if they hold nothing of value.

It will take a little while getting used to wild card video poker after playing the non-wild versions, but once you get accustomed you should have a lot of fun at these machines.

Summary of Winning Strategy

Video poker is certainly a fun game, for it is a game of skill, and as we stated in the beginning, with proper play you can have the edge over the casino. Like blackjack, you'll need to study the correct strategies carefully to come out a winner.

For those players serious about winning money at video poker, the professional video poker strategy advertised in the back is highly recommended. You'll learn the important differences in strategy between the 8-5 Progressive and 9-6 Jacks or Better machines, and receive complete strategy charts for these games, the wild card games, and others.

Meanwhile, use your skill to good advantage, and see if you can't beat the house and be a winner!

WINNING AT CARIBBEAN STUD POKER

INTRODUCTION

Caribbean Stud Poker is similar to standard poker in that both share the common rankings of the hands, however, it is dissimilar in that the game is played against the dealer, not the other players at the table. Additionally, there is none of the bluffing and skillful play that is an integral part of regular poker.

The game is relatively simple to play. Like five card stud poker, five cards will be received by each participating player - there will be no draws. The player's only decisions are whether to call an additional bet after several cards are dealt, or whether to fold the hand and forfeit the original ante bet.

There is one other facet to the game that entices players to the Caribbean Stud Poker tables: There is a progressive jackpot that pays off as much as hundreds of thousands of dollars if a royal flush is drawn, and smaller bonus payouts for other winning hands.

THE BASICS OF CARIBBEAN STUD POKER

The Layout

Caribbean Stud Poker is played on a table that closely resembles that of a blackjack table, with the players seated around the oval side of the table, and the dealer standing along the flat side facing the players. In front of the dealer is a chip rack holding the table's bankroll. It is from this rack that the dealer will pay off winning hands, or deposit losing bets that he has collected.

The table is usually built to accommodate seven players seated around the oval side, along with corresponding betting areas on the layout. The game can be played with just one player against the dealer or with the full complement of seven players. In either case, it doesn't affect the strategy or play of Caribbean Stud Poker, for players play against the house not against each other.

The Cards

The standard 52 card pack is used in Caribbean Stud Poker, with 13 cards of each rank, Ace to King, and four suits, spades, diamonds, clubs, and hearts. The game is usually dealt from a single deck of cards using the Shuffle Master shuffling machine, an increasingly popular device used by the casinos that automatically shuffles the cards. The Shuffle Master machine is always found to the dealers left, or from the players vantage point, on the right side of the table.

The Betting Spots

In front of each player's position are three betting spots, one for each of the three bets a player can make. The first spot, closest to the player and in a circle, is marked "bet", the second spot, rectangular in shape, is marked "ante". The final betting area, closest to the dealer, is actually a drop slot, a "hole" in the table where a $1 coin or chip gets deposited to participate in the progressive jackpot.

WINNING AT CARIBBEAN STUD POKER

The Object of The Game

The players goal in Caribbean Stud Poker is to draw a five card poker hand that is stronger than the dealer's qualifying hand, and also, when good cards are drawn, to hold a hand that is strong enough to qualify for a bonus payout. The higher ranking the player's hand, the greater the bonus won, with the caveat that the dealer must possess a qualifying hand for the bonus to count. We'll see what this means later on.

When placing the $1 optional progressive wager in Caribbean Stud Poker, the player's goal for that bet is to draw a flush or better to receive additional bonus payouts. In particular, the player would like to get a Royal Flush, a hand that can win him hundreds of thousands of dollars.

Before we look at qualifying hands, and how that affects the game, we'll review the poker hands for players unfamiliar with their rankings.

Ranks of the Hands

Following are the valid poker hands used in Caribbean Stud Poker. Hands are listed in order of strength, from the most powerful, the royal flush, to the least powerful, the hands less than A K high, which are all of equally poor value in this game.

All hands are poker hands recognized in regular high poker.

Royal Flush - An A K Q J 10, all of the same suit is called a royal flush. For example, A K Q J 10 of spades is a royal flush. The odds of being dealt a royal flush, the best hand possible in Caribbean Stud Poker, is one in 649,740.

Straight Flush - Five cards of the same suit in numerical sequence, such as the J 10 9 8 7 of clubs, is called a straight flush. This particular example is called a jack high straight flush since the jack is the highest ranking card. The ace must be used as either the highest card in the straight flush (an ace high straight flush is actually a royal flush) or the lowest card, as in A 2 3 4 5 of diamonds, to be valid. The hand of Q K A 2 3 of clubs is not a straight flush, simply a flush only.

Four of a Kind - Four cards of identical rank, such as the hand 6 6 6 6 3, is called a four of a kind. The odd card in the above example, the 3, is irrelevant and has no bearing on the rank of the hand.

Full House - A full house consists of three cards of identical rank along with two cards of an identical but different rank. 8 8 8 J J and K K K 7 7 are two examples of a full house.

Flush - Any five cards of the same suit constitutes a flush in poker. A K 7 3 2 of spades is an ace high flush in spades and Q 10 7 5 3 of hearts is a queen high flush in hearts.

Straight - Five non-suited cards in sequential order, such as 10 9 8 7 6, are a straight. When straights contain an ace, the ace must serve as either the highest card in the run, such as the ace high straight A K Q J 10, or the lowest card, as in the five high straight, 5 4 3 2 A. The cards Q K A 2 3 is not a straight. It is merely an ace high hand and will be beaten by any pair.

Three of a Kind - Three matched cards of identical value along with two odd cards (unmatched) are called a three of a kind. 7 7 7 Q 2 is an example of three of a kind.

Two Pair - Two sets of equivalently valued or "paired" cards along with an unmatched card, is a two pair hand. 4 4 3 3 A and K K 3 3 J are examples of two pair hands.

One Pair - One set of identically valued cards along with three unmatched cards are called a pair. The hand 2 2 8 4 A is referred to as "a pair of twos". Pairs are ranked in order of value from Aces, the highest, down to the deuces, the lowest. Thus, a pair of aces beats out a pair of kings, and a pair of nines wins over a pair of sixes.

Ace-King Hand - The next ranking hand in Caribbean Stud Poker is the hand lacking all above combinations but led by an Ace and a King, such as the hand A K J 5 3. This is the minimum strength hand that would be deemed a qualifying dealer hand. If both the dealer and the player hold this hand, then the highest-ranked of the remaining odd cards ranks supreme.

All Other Hands - Any hand not including any of the above combinations is a non-qualifying hand and has no value in Caribbean Stud Poker.

Odds of Drawing Hands

Following is a table showing the odds of getting dealt winning hands in Caribbean Stud Poker. These are the same odds as those in regular draw poker for the first five cards dealt.

ODDS OF DRAWING WINNING HANDS

Royal Flush	649,739 -1
Straight Flush	72,192 -1
Four of a Kind	4,165 -1
Full House	693 -1
Flush	508 -1
Straight	254 -1
Three of a Kind	46 -1
Two Pair	20 -1
One Pair	1.37 -1

Resolving Tied Hands

Should both the dealer and player be dealt equivalently ranked hands, then the normal rules of poker rankings would apply to determine the more powerful hand, and therefore the winner. This typically involves using the higher ranked odd cards to determine the better hand, or in the case of flush and straight type hands, the highest cards leading those hands.

THE PLAY OF THE GAME

Before any action can take place, participating players must make their initial bets. To begin the betting, each player must place at least the minimum bet in the area marked ante. The minimum and maximum bets allowable will usually be posted on a small placard in the corner of the table.

In the typical casino, $5 will be the minimum bet allowed as ante. Players may also choose to make the Progressive Bet by dropping $1 into the drop slot. For now, no money can be wagered in the area marked "bet".

Once all players are ready to go and have placed their bets in the area marked ante, the dealer is ready to get the action going. The dealer's first action is to push a button that will automatically collect the $1 progressive bets that were made. These bets will drop out of sight into the bowels of the table and a red light will go on in front of each player who made the bet to indicate that that bet was made. The ante bets will still remain as before.

The dealer is now ready to distribute the cards. Five cards will be dealt face down to each participating player. The dealer will also deal himself five cards, four face down and one face up to be viewed by all players. This face up card is known as the upcard.

Players now have a decision to make about their hand. If they feel it is good enough to beat the dealer or qualify for a bonus payout, they can call, and do so by placing an additional wager in the box marked bet. This wager must be double the ante bet. Thus, if $5 was bet as an ante, then $10 would be placed in the bet area. Similarly, if $25 was the ante, then $50 would be the additional wager placed in the bet area. In the first case, the player would have total ante and call bets of $15, and in the second case, adding $25 to $50, $75 would be the total.

To indicate that the player wishes to make this additional bet, the player places his cards face down on the table. Players that do not wish to place this additional bet must fold, and do so by returning their cards to the dealer. While their ante bet is forfeited and collected by the house, no additional money is at risk for the hand. Players that have folded no longer participate in the hand.

Each player in turn will make the decision to play on by placing the additional double bet in the "call" box, or to fold and forfeit their ante bet. This is the only playing decision players will make once the cards are dealt. Play will proceed clockwise, beginning with the player at the dealer's left (the players right side) and continuing on to the third base position, the player positioned at the dealer's far right.

Once all players have made their decisions, the dealer will turn over his remaining four down cards to reveal his final five card hand. This hand will determine whether players have won or lost on their bets. The dealer first sees if he has a qualifying hand, the minimum hand required by the rules of the game to determine if bonuses and extra payouts will occur to players with stronger hands.

The Qualifying Hand

A qualifying hand is one in which the dealer has at least an Ace and a King, or a higher total such as a pair or better for his five cards. For example, A K 4 3 2 (Ace-King high), 3 3 7 9 Q (pair of threes), and 7 8 9 10 J (straight), are all qualifying dealer hands, while A Q 3 4 7 is not.

Why is a qualifying hand so important? We'll take a look at that now.

When the Dealer Does Not Have a Qualifying Hand

If the dealer does not have a qualifying hand, then all players who have remained in the game win their Ante bet, regardless of whether that hand is stronger than the player's.

For example, if the dealer holds A J 10 8 2, a non-qualifying hand, and the player holds Q 9 8 6 2 or even 7 6 4 3 2, the player wins. The dealer cannot win if his hand doesn't contain at least a hand of A K strength. Players who folded however, have already conceded defeat and lost their bets. But for players who made call bets (anyone who didn't make a call bet had to have folded), a non-qualifying dealer hand spells an automatic winning hand.

That's the good news. The bad news is that if the dealer does not have a qualifying hand, players win *only* the Ante bet. Their call bets, the ones placed in the bet area, are returned to them. They are not eligible for any Bonus payouts or even 1-1 payoffs regardless of the hand drawn. That's the tough part of the game.

Thus, if $5 was wagered on the Ante and $10 in the Bet circle, and the player happened to hold three Jacks, the total win would be only $5, the $5 paid at even money for the won ante bet. The non-qualifying dealer hand negates the 3-1 bonus that would have been paid for the three of a kind if that player's hand was stronger than the dealer's. In the above example, the $10 wager in the Bet circle would be returned.

If the dealer does have a qualifying hand, there is no automatic win. Now, the stronger hand between the dealer and the player is the deciding factor. Let's see how this works.

When the Dealer Has a Qualifying Hand

When the dealer does have that qualifying hand though, that is, at least an A K or better hand, than he'll compare his hand to each of the players to see who has the stronger hand.

As opposed to the non-qualifying situation, both the ante bet and the call bet (the wager in the "bet" area) are at stake now. The player will either win both bets or lose both, depending upon whether he has a stronger total, which would be a winner, or a weaker total, which would be a loser.

For example, if $5 were bet on the ante and $10 on the call bet, and the dealer held two jacks to the players two deuces, than the player would lose both bets for a total $15 loss since, of course, two jacks are a stronger hand than two deuces.

However, if the player has the better hand, than both bets are won instead. Each wager, the ante bet and the call bet is paid differently. Ante bets are paid at even money, 1-1, while call bets are paid according to a bonus schedule which we'll show below.

BONUS PAYOUTS ON THE CALL BET	
Royal Flush	100-1
Straight Flush	50-1
Four of a Kind	20-1
Full House	7-1
Flush	5-1
Straight	4-1
Three of a Kind	3-1
Two Pair	2-1
One Pair	1-1

We'll look at an example hand to make the bonus payouts perfectly clear.

Let's say we have a $5 Ante bet, and of course, our call bet, which is double, is $10. We receive three of a kind and the dealer holds a pair of Aces. We'll win $5 for the Ante bet, plus $30 on the $10 call bet (three of a kind paid at 3-1) for a total win of $35. This would be in addition to the original $15 in bets that were made, $5 on the ante and $10 on the call. Thus, $50 would be returned to us.

We would not qualify for the bonus payout in the unlucky event that the dealer doesn't hold a qualifying hand. Only the ante bet would be won. We also don't qualify for bonus payouts if the dealer holds a stronger hand than our hand. In that case, not only is there no bonus payout on the call bet, but both the ante and call bets are outright losers.

Note that the dealer only wins at even money, regardless of the strength of his hand and that bonus payouts for the players are made only on the call bet itself and not on the ante.

THE MAXIMUM BONUS PAYOUT

Players must be aware that casinos have a limit on the maximum amount they'll pay winners on the Bonus Payouts. Some limits may be as low as $5,000 (even lower ones might be found), while others might go as high as $50,000 or more. This limit will be posted on the table and may read, "Bonus payouts may not exceed table's maximum payout."

How does this affect the player? Well, not in a good way if the player gets a big hand and is denied the full payout because it exceeds the maximum posted table limit. Let's look at an example. Say the player has wagered $150 on the call bet and draws a straight flush in a casino with a $5,000 Bonus Payout. Normally the player would be entitled to $7,500 (50-1 x the $150 bet). However, since the maximum bonus payout is only $5,000, the player loses out on the extra $2,500 - a big hit to take. The "penalty" would be even worse if that hand was a royal flush paying 100-1 on the bonus; now the player would only get $5,000 of the $15,000, losing out on the extra $10,000!

To protect against losing out on the full amount that should be paid on a bonus payout, players must always make sure that the maximum call bet multiplied by 100 does not exceed the bonus payout. We use the number 100 because the largest bonus, on the royal flush, pays at 100-1. If 100 multiplied by a player's call bet is greater than the casino's limit, then the drawing of a royal flush would not get the full payout. As we've just shown, it will exceed that limit.

To easily come up with the maximum bet that won't be penalized if a royal flush is drawn, divide the casino's maximum payout by 100. For example, if the maximum payout is $5,000, dividing it by 100, the player's maximum call bet should not exceed $50. And of course, if the call bet is $50, the ante, which is always half that amount, would be $25.

Or, if a player likes to think in terms of the ante, which is half of the call bet, then the maximum casino payout limit should be divided by 200 to find the largest ante bet that should be made. Using the $5,000 casino limit example above, and dividing by 200, gives us an answer of a $25 maximum ante bet that should be made, and of course, a maximum $50 call bet since that bet is always double the ante bet.

No surprise; that's the same $25 ante and $50 call bets we figured before, but came to from a different direction.

If a player likes to bet at much higher numbers, then casinos should be sought out that provide their patrons with higher maximum payouts.

THE PROGRESSIVE JACKPOT

The optional wager we spoke about earlier, the Progressive bet, is made by placing $1 in the drop slot or progressive slot as it is also known, before the cards are dealt. The goal of this bet is to draw a flush or higher ranked hand to receive additional bonus payouts. While flushes, full houses, and other powerful hands would be great, what the player really would like to get is a royal flush, a hand that will win the full progressive amount.

Near each Caribbean Stud Poker table is a Jackpot Meter that goes up in value each time $1 is placed into the drop slot by any table linked up to that meter within the casino. This jackpot can be as little as $5,000 or $10,000, the general starting point after a royal flush is hit, depending upon the casino, or as high as hundreds and hundreds of thousands of dollars.

Every time prior to dealing the cards that the dealer pushes the button which collects the progressive bets, the jackpot will go up its percentage in value, and get that much sweeter. The amount each progressive bet increases the jackpot varies from casino to casino. Some casinos put in only 49¢ of each dollar played, while others, particularly larger more forward thinking casinos that understand the value of larger jackpots to draw players, may put in as much as 75¢ per dollar played to boost the jackpots faster. Obviously, the smaller the amount of money put back into the progressive, the slower the jackpot will grow.

However, the actual percentage of money that gets put back into the jackpot is not really a concern for us as players; we only care who has the highest jackpots if we're going to play for them. How they got that high is neither here nor there. How high? That is the only question we need to know. It will be no coincidence that more aggressive casinos will tend to have the highest jackpots.

As that jackpot grows, so does player interest. It's just like the lottery. The larger the jackpot, the greater the players' appetites to try and win that prize.

What does it take to win the full amount of the progressive? Why, nothing less than the big sandwich with all the dressings itself - the royal flush. While drawing this hand would certainly be nice, a player shouldn't hold his or her breath - it's a longshot. As we saw in the earlier chart, the odds of hitting the royal flush is 1 in 649,739. But playing longshots is what much of gambling is about anyway.

There are other paying hands as well in the Progressive Jackpot. The charts on the following page show two payout schedules that a player might find. The first schedule, which might be found at a few larger casinos aggressively going after Caribbean Stud Poker players, is a liberal payout schedule that works for the benefit for the player.

The second schedule, which is more commonly found, pays much less on the four of a kind, full house, and flush hands, and that of course, is to the detriment of the player.

LIBERAL PAYOUT SCHEDULE (A)
500/250/100

Royal Flush	100% of the Jackpot
Straight Flush	10% of the Jackpot
Four of a Kind	$500
Full House	$250
Flush	$100

COMMON PAYOUT SCHEDULE (B)
100/75/50

Royal Flush	100% of the Jackpot
Straight Flush	10% of the Jackpot
Four of a Kind	$100
Full House	$75
Flush	$50

There are other payout schedules you'll find. In between the 500/250/100 liberal schedule shown above, and the 100/75/50 also shown, you may find 500/150/75, 500/100/75, 500/100/50, 500/75/50,

300/100/50, 250/100/50, and 150/100/50. The three numbers for each group stand respectively for the four of a kind, full house and flush payoffs.

You should keep in mind that the progressive is a separate bet and is not affected by the results of the ante or regular call bet. For example, if the player draws a full house and the dealer miraculously (or is it disastrously?) has a four of a kind at the same time, the player would still win $250 on the $1 progressive bet (assuming the more liberal payout schedule shown) even though the call and ante bets are losers.

By the same token, the player gets the full bonus payout on the $1 progressive bet even if the dealer doesn't have a qualifying hand. Thus, players must be careful to alert the dealers to their flush or better hands when the dealer has a non-qualifying hand in case the dealer accidentally removes the cards before checking for progressive winners.

There is no maximum limit on a progressive payout as there is with the bonus payout. If the royal flush is hit, players will get paid the full amount of the progressive meter.

Aggregate Payoff on Progressives

One other casino rule comes into play on the Progressive payout. The Bonus Payout is limited to an *Aggregate* payoff on the straight flush and the royal flush. What this means is that on a straight flush hand for example, a total of 10% will be paid out. Thus, if two players hold a straight flush on the same deal, they would split that 10%, in effect, getting only 5% each.

If the meter showed $12,000, the total pool of $1,200 for the straight flush would be divided evenly between the two winners at $600 each. This applies only to straight flush and royal flush hands on progressive wagers, not to the bonus payouts on the four of a kind, full house and flush hands, where each player will receive the full amount listed.

The chances of two players holding a straight or royal flush on the very same hand is so unlikely, quantum degrees more than one hundred million to 1 against (the exact odds depending upon how many other players are at the table), that this casino rule shouldn't be of great concern to you.

HOUSE PERCENTAGE

The odds in Caribbean Stud Poker for the ante bets are similar to American double zero roulette, which is to say, they are not kind to the player. With proper strategy, the player is trying to buck a house edge of about 5.25%, difficult odds to overcome for players trying to beat the game. If the call bets are included, the house edge drops to 2.56%. Let me explain this a bit further.

The call bets in Caribbean Stud Poker, similar to double downs in blackjack or odds bets in craps, are only placed when the player either has an even game against the house, or actually has an edge. A player never wants to increase the size of a wager or put additional money attached to a wager when there are negative expectations involved. That is counter-intuitive to a winning approach.

On average, with proper strategy, a player will make a call bet half the time, actually about 52% of the time.

To look at it another way, every second hand will involve a call bet, which is a double bet. For example, if the ante is $5, the call bet is double that, or $10. Thus, if we simulate a progression, the first bet will total one bet, the second bet will total three bets (the ante and double call bet), the third bet will be the ante bet, the fourth bet will be the three bets again, and so on.

When we add together each set of bets, we average approximately two bets per hand.

Just looking at the ante bet by itself, a player will lose at a 5.26% clip. However, when the call bets are averaged in, which when played correctly are profitable for the player, the overall house odds drop to 2.56% of the money wagered.

If we compare these odds to baccarat, craps, and blackjack, games which offer much superior odds - 1.36% in baccarat, on banker and player wages, .08% or .06% in craps if the proper bets are placed, or even an outright advantage in blackjack with correct play - and you'll understand why I'm not so hot on this table game.

At more than a 5% disadvantage on the ante bet, or 2.56% when the call bets are averaged in, players will see their bankrolls steadily bleed dry as the hours tick on and the hands get dealt. It's a relatively large house edge the way I see it, and if players try their hand long enough, they'll start to see things the way I do.

However, if players enjoy the game, and are excited by the possibilities, well, that's what gambling is all about. Gamblers could do much worse at keno, Big Six and the slots machines. As long as players realize that they're up against a big take compared to the other table games, then the game can be approached with open eyes.

On the good side, Caribbean Stud Poker is like all other gambling games; players will have their good streaks and bad streaks. With a little luck and smart money management, players can emerge with winnings in the short run.

WINNING STRATEGIES

Playing Strategy

There is one crucial decision to make in Caribbean Stud Poker and that is whether to make the call wager at double the ante size, or to fold and forfeit the ante without exposing additional money to risk. In some cases, as when players have a strong hand such as three of a kind or two pairs, the strategy is fairly obvious–we want the additional money out there. On the other hand, when our cards are weak and we don't even have an A and a K, cards that will at least compete with a qualifying dealer total, the strategy is also clearcut –we'll want to fold.

The basic strategy we show below will have players playing at a near optimal level. Playing the absolute perfect optimal strategy will gain players so little as to be negligible; only a few hundredths of a percent can be gained with perfect playing strategy. It is so tiny a gain, especially when we're dealing with a negative expectation of over five percent to begin with, that the extra effort needed to learn a semi-complicated playing strategy is not worth it by any stretch of the imagination. Players need not even worry about it; the strategy presented here is all that a player needs to know.

The correct playing strategy divides hands into those which are stronger than the dealer's qualifying total of A K, which we'll generally keep, and hands which are weaker than the minimum A K, which we'll throw away and surrender the ante.

We'll look at the details below starting with the strongest hands, and work our way down to the weakest hands.

• **Two Pair or Higher**. Two pair, three and four of a kind, straights, flushes, full houses, and straight and royal flushes are all very strong hands that not only are heavily favored to win, but which pay bonus payouts. The strategy for this grouping of hands is very clear even to beginning players - make the call bet!

• **Pairs**. Pairs are dealt 42% of the time in five card poker, so this is a hand players will see on a regular basis. The correct strategy when holding a pair, any pair, is to call, regardless of the dealer's upcard. This is a clear gain in all situations.

Note that this doesn't mean players win money in the long run in all pair situations. For example, when holding 2's, 3's, 4's, 5's, 6's, and 7's, players long term expectations are negative, that is, they will show a loss. However, except for the lowest of pairs, the 2's-4's, players will always have a positive expectation of winning when their pair is greater than the dealer's upcard.

Our strategy with these low pairs is to minimize losses, just as in blackjack when we are dealt inferior hands like 12-16 - the bust hands. In Caribbean Stud Poker, it is a mistake to throw away small pairs just because they're weak.

The strongest pairs are 10's, J's, Q's, K's, and A's. These pairs have a positive expectation of winning against all dealer upcards.

• **A K vs. Dealer**. When we hold A K, we have a borderline hand whose strategy depends on the other three cards we hold, and the dealer's upcard. This is a special strategy situation based on the qualifying dealer rules of the minimum A K hand.

Following are the two breakdowns for playing A K hands.

1. When our third highest card is a J or Q, we call the dealer.

For example, the hand A K J 9 4 should be played against all dealer upcards including the A.

The thinking here is that if the dealer makes a qualifying hand of A K x x x, x standing for any other non-pairing (or cards which form a higher hand), the A K J or better hand is strong enough to win, thus making the call bet a profitable play.

2. When our third highest card is less than a J, we call the dealer only if his upcard matches one of our five up cards; otherwise we fold.

Examples: Call with A K 10 5 2 vs. A, and vs. 2, but fold A K 10 5 2 vs. Q, and A K 8 7 6 vs. 5.

The Ace-King hands are close plays that, percentage wise, are almost 50-50 for the player in terms of long term gain. To make calling a correct play, that is, a theoretical gain over not calling and folding, we need the little extra edge that favors our hand. In the situation where one of our cards matches the dealer's upcard, the dealer is that much less likely to have a pair and defeat us. There is now one less card that can help the dealer.

• **A Q or Less vs. Dealer.** Any hand that doesn't have at least an A K or better should be folded. For example, fold these cards: A Q J 10 9,

A Q 8 7 6, K Q J 10 6, and 10 8 4 3 2.

In all cases, if the dealer qualifies, these hands are losers. Obviously, since a qualifying dealer hand, by definition, contains an A K or better, it beats all the hands in this category.

The Disadvantage of Playing AQ or Lesser Hands

There is one constant in Caribbean Stud Poker that will make the playing of A Q or less hands disastrous: The dealer will make a qualifying hand approximately 56% of the time. At first glance, you might think that the loss is $12 for every $100 bet - 56 losses less 44 wins.

That's a very convincing argument not to make this play. Giving up 12% is enormous and a foolish play. But the loss is much worse! It's equivalent to being more than ten times worse than that, about 125% when based on the ante bet! Let's take a closer look.

Here's how the math breaks down.

We'll use a $10 ante bet for this example. Of the 44 times the dealer doesn't qualify, we win a total of only $440. Since the dealer didn't qualify, only the ante bet is paid off. The $20 call bet is returned. That's $10 for each winning hand at 1-1, even money. Of the other 56 times that the dealer qualifies, we not only lose the $10 ante bet, but the $20 call bet as well! That's $1680 in losses against only $440 in wins for a net loss of $1240.

Thus for every $1,000 made in Ante bets, a loss of $1240 is 124%, actually closer to 125% (we rounded down the 56% number to show the math easier). That's a pretty heavy loss to try and beat in this game.

Making these kind of plays will destroy a player at the table. Players should never, ever think about playing these type of hands. These horrible plays are worse than any other play that can be found in the entire casino and that's pretty bad. To be a winner at Caribbean Stud Poker, you absolutely must avoid any situation that give the house an exorbitant edge.

PROGRESSIVE $1 BET STRATEGY

Generally speaking, unless the progressive jackpot is in the hundreds of thousands, the progressive $1 wager is a complete sucker bet giving the house an edge that hovers around 50% in most cases and goes as high as almost 75% in the worse case. Ouch!

Even when the jackpot is say $250,000, the player still may be giving the casino an enormous edge by making this bet. The exact edge the casino enjoys is a function of several factors - the actual bonus paid on four of a kinds, full houses and flushes, which as we've seen, varies from casino to casino; the size of the jackpot itself; and equally important, the size of the ante bet.

This last factor, the size of the ante bet, is important because the progressive bet cannot be made as an independent wager by itself. At a minimum, to play Caribbean Stud Poker, the player must place an ante bet, and then optionally, if desired, he or she can make the progressive bet as well. Since each bet gives the casino roughly a 5.25% edge, the larger the average bet, the higher the jackpot must be to compensate for these bets.

If a player feels the pressing need to make that $1 "dream" bet, he might consider the lottery. Lousy odds, but if the player does hit, the payout is not a few measly tens of thousands of dollars, it's a two year cruise around the world, a dream home, instant retirement, and the most expensive cigars money can buy.

But then again, my advice is always to play with grounded rationale. Make the best bets the games can give you, and if winning, make sure to walk away with the casino money in your pocket.

BETTING STRATEGY

In Caribbean Stud Poker, there is no particular betting strategy to pursue in terms of gaining an advantage as there is in blackjack, except to bet intelligently according to one's bankroll.

Occasionally, the progressive jackpot may get into the hundreds of thousands of dollars, and the bettor will be looking at a positive expectation on the progressive $1 wager. This is rarely seen, but in these instances, when we're chasing a very large progressive jackpot, a situation which actually gives us the edge, our strategy will be to keep the ante bet as small as possible to minimize the effect of the house edge on the ante and call bets.

OVERALL WINNING STRATEGY

The main thing to keep in mind with Caribbean Stud Poker is that the game is a negative expectation gamble. The casino has an advantage of 5.25% on the regular ante bets, 2,56% when the call bets are taken into account.

Theoretically, the longer a bettor plays, the closer to the 5.25% and 2.56% "taxes" that will be extracted by the inevitable house edge built-in to the game. On the progressive bet, as we discussed earlier, the house edge can soar to almost 75%, or in exceptionable cases, where the progressive jackpot is in the hundreds of thousands of dollars, can actually favor the player. But as we all know, there are up and down swings in gambling. Anyone, with a little luck, can walk away from the table a winner. But to maximize one's chances of winning, bettors must play their cards correctly and make only the best bets available to them.

A player's first order of business is to avoid the progressive bet. Unless the jackpot is enormous, at least $200,000 or more, depending upon the circumstances, this bet gives too much away to the casino. Avoiding this wager will avoid a constant drain on a player's bankroll.

Secondly, bettors must study the playing strategy so that the correct moves are made and the chances of winning are optimized. As we saw earlier, there is a lot of information to remember, but one must learn the strategies and use them all the time, not just when the mood strikes.

There is no substitute for correct play. Hunches only build the casinos bigger and make the players poorer.

Finally, intelligent money management decisions must be employed at the tables. When things are going poorly, which they sometimes do, we must limit our losses. We will never take a bad beating in any one session. And when we're on a hot streak, we'll make sure that we leave a winner.

We'll never give the casino back all our winnings once we've got a big winning streak going. That's not only the key in Caribbean Stud Poker, but in all gambling pursuits.

WINNING
AT
LET IT RIDE

INTRODUCTION

Let it Ride was first introduced to the Las Vegas casinos in August, 1993, and can now be found in hundreds of casinos across the country as well as in international casinos as well. The Shuffle Master company, developer of Let it Ride, Let it Ride: The Tournament, and Let it Ride Bonus, has attracted many players to this game.

Why the big fuss? Well, for one, Let it Ride offers players thousands of dollars in prizes if the optional $1 bonus bet is made and a big hand is drawn. That's always attractive to gamblers.

Second, Let it Ride, like Caribbean Stud Poker, draws some of it's popularity from its similarities with poker, a game familiar to gamblers. Thus, players find Let it Ride easy to learn and play.

And third, the unique aspect of the game that lets players remove two of their three bets when they're unhappy with the cards they're dealt, is a feature that strikes a responsive chord among players.

BEGINNER'S GUIDE TO LET IT RIDE

The Basics of Play

Let it Ride is a simplified version of five card poker. Players get dealt three cards, and use these in combination with the two community cards shared by all players to form a final five card hand that either qualifies for a payout, which is a winner, or is of lesser value, which is a loser.

There are no draws of additional cards, bluffing of opponents, or strategy decisions other than deciding whether to take down two of the three mandatory starting bets in the game, or whether to let them ride. Unlike other table games offered by the casino, players do not compete against a dealer or other players, winning hands are solely judged according to the strength of the five card total as it relates to the paytable.

The Layout

Let it Ride is played on a blackjack-style table with a single standard pack of 52 cards. On the flat side of the table is the dealer who performs all the functions one would expect; the dealing of the cards, the paying off and collection of won and lost bets, and the overall running of the game. In front of the dealer will be the chip rack, where the bankroll of the table sits in long colorful rows in full view of the players.

Across from the dealer, along the oval edge and facing him, are as many as seven participating players, trying their hand with lady luck.

On the layout itself, where the game is played and all bets are made, are three betting circles in front of each player's seat. These circles are laid out next to each other, horizontally, in front of each player's position. Going left to right, they are marked **"1"**, **"2"** and **"$"** respectively. These are the spots where the three mandatory bets are placed by each participating player.

There is one additional bet spot as well, a red button located in front of each player, where an optional $1 wager can be made on Let it Ride, The Tournament, or the new bet which has replaced the Tournament bet almost everywhere, the Let it Ride Bonus Bet.

Another item on the table might be the Shuffle Master shuffling machine, an increasingly popular device that automatically shuffles the cards.

The Object of the Game

The player's goal in Let it Ride is to draw a hand that is strong enough to qualify for one of the winners in the payout schedule. These payoffs range in value from even money wins, 1-1 on a tens or better pair, to 1000-1 when the Royal Flush is hit.

When placing the $1 optional wager on Let it Ride, The Tournament, a player's additional goal is to get a straight flush or a royal flush, hands that not only pay $2,000 or $20,000 respectively, but enter that player in the big tournament which has a grand prize of one million dollars when this $1 bet is made. In the Let it Ride Bonus game the lure is a payoff as high as $10,000 or $25,000, depending upon the venue.

There is no competition against other players as in regular poker, or against the dealer as in Caribbean Stud Poker. In Let it Ride, the goal is solely to draw a hand strong enough to qualify for a payout.

Hands That Qualify For Payouts

As we mentioned above, the player's goal is to draw a hand that qualifies for a winning payout. The higher the rank of the hand, the greater the payout. At a minimum, a player must have a tens or better payout to be a winner. Any lesser hand fails to qualify for a payout, and the player's bets will be lost.

The best hand, the royal flush pays 1,000 to 1 in most of the casinos that offer the game. There are jurisdictions where the gaming commission has mandated that the highest payoff, that of the royal flush, be at the smaller 500-1, or where casinos have chosen this paytable for their customer.

The following charts show the winning hands and payoffs for the two basic paytables that will be found.

Typical Payoff Schedule

The following paytable is the standard one found in casinos, and features a 1000-1 payoff on a royal flush. The players get compensated more for big wins on this schedule, and less for the full house and flush wins, as we'll see.

TYPICAL PAYOFF SCHEDULE	
Royal Flush	1,000-1
Straight Flush	200-1
Four of a Kind	50-1
Full House	11-1
Flush	8-1
Straight	5-1
Three of a Kind	3-1
Two Pair	2-1
Pair of 10's or Better	1-1

Alternate Payoff Schedule

This is the other basic payoff schedule that is found in some locations. While the player receives a smaller payoff on the less frequent winners, the flush, straight flush, royal flush, and four of a kind hands, you'll see that the payoffs for the more frequently hit full house and flush hands are greater.

Either payoff chart, however, will give the player equivalent odds.

ALTERNATE PAYOFF SCHEDULE

Hand	Payoff
Royal Flush	500-1
Straight Flush	100-1
Four of a Kind	25-1
Full House	15-1
Flush	10-1
Straight	5-1
Three of a Kind	3-1
Two Pair	2-1
Pair of 10's or Better	1-1

THE WINNING POKER HANDS

For players unfamiliar with poker, or who want to brush up on their knowledge of poker combinations, we've listed the categories of valid poker hands recognized in Let it Ride. Hands are listed in order of strength, from the most powerful, the royal flush, to the least powerful, the hands which don't qualify for a payout at all.

Royal Flush - An A, K, Q, J and 10, all of the same suit is a royal flush. For example, A, K, Q, J 10, of spades, is a royal flush.

Straight Flush - Five cards of the same suit in numerical sequence, such as the J 10 9 8 7 of clubs, is called a straight flush. The ace must be used as either the highest card in the straight flush (an ace high one being a royal flush) or the lowest card, as in A 2 3 4 5 of diamonds, to be valid. The hand of Q K A 2 3 of clubs is not a straight flush, simply a flush only.

Four of a Kind - Four cards of identical rank, such as the hand 6 6 6 6 3, is called a four of a kind. The odd card in the above example, the 3, is irrelevant and has no bearing on the rank of the hand.

Full House - A full house consists of three cards of identical rank along with two cards of an identical but different rank. 8 8 8 J J and K K K 7 7 are two examples of a full house.

Flush - Any five cards of the same suit constitutes a flush in poker. A K 7 3 2 of spades is called an ace high flush in spades and Q 10 7 5 3 of hearts is a queen high flush in hearts.

Straight - Five non-suited cards in sequential order, such as 10 9 8 7 6, are called a straight. When straights contain an ace, the ace must serve as either the highest card in the run, such as the ace high straight A K Q J 10, or the lowest card, as in the five high straight, 5 4 3 2 A. The cards Q K A 2 3 of mixed suits is not a straight. It is merely an ace high hand.

Three of a Kind - Three matched cards of identical value along with two odd cards (unmatched) are called a three of a kind. 7 7 7 Q 2 is an example of three of a kind.

Two Pair - Two sets of equivalently valued or "paired" cards along with an unmatched card, are called two pairs. 4 4 3 3 A and K K 3 3 J are examples of two pair hands.

Tens or Better - One set of identically valued cards along with three unmatched cards are called a pair. The hand J J 7 4 2 is a pair of jacks. In Let it Ride, the minimum hand that qualifies for a payout is a pair of tens or higher. Thus, tens, jacks, queens, kings, and aces, are all winning totals with the 1-1 payout. Pairs of nines and lesser strength pairs don't qualify for payouts.

All Other Hands - Any hand not including any of the above combinations is a losing hand with no payouts, and thus, has no value in the regular Let it Ride table game.

THE PLAY OF THE GAME

Before any cards are dealt, participating players at the table must make a bet on each of the three betting circles in front of them. These bets must be made in equal amounts. For example, if $5 were to be bet on the circle marked "1", then that same $5 must be bet on the other two circles, the one marked "2", and the one marked "$".

Additionally, a $1 wager may be made on the Tournament or Bonus spot. We'll go over this bet in a little bit.

There is normally a minimum $5 bet on each circle, though smaller casinos may offer minimums as low as $3. In the first case, a minimum of $15 total would have to be bet among three bet circles, $5 per spot, and in the second case, a minimum of $9, $3 per spot, would be required.

Once all players have completed betting, and the cards are shuffled and ready to go, the dealer will deal three down cards to each player. The dealer will also deal two face down cards and place them in the two rectangular boxes imprinted on the layout in front of his position. These cards are called community cards, and will be shared by all active players to form their final five card holding.

The rules of the game disallow players from showing their cards to their fellow players at the table. The casinos don't want players to gain any untoward advantage that may help them make better playing decisions. (This is unlike regular poker where sharing card information actually hurt's a player's chance of winning since he plays against the other players at the table.)

At Let it Ride, players strategize only their own hand's winning chances. The relative strengths of other players hands has no bearing on a player's own chances of winning, though the cards those hands contain may help provide information to a player's own playing decision.

Beginning with the player on the dealer's left and proceeding in a clockwise direction, each player in turn has the following options:

The Player's First Option

Each player in turn, after looking at his or her three down cards, has the option of playing for the bet in circle "1", that is, letting it ride, or withdrawing that bet from play and having it returned to his or her bankroll.

Letting a bet ride is done by placing the cards under or in front of the cards in the circle marked "1". The dealer will understand this motion to mean that the player wishes to keep his or her bet in play, and will move on to the next player.

A player that wishes to remove his or her bet from play, does so by simply scraping the table with the cards. This motion will prompt the dealer to remove that player's bet from the first circle and return it to the player. Thus, any player who is unhappy with the cards dealt to him, is able to remove his or her bet from the circle marked "1".

Players should not physically take back their own bets; they should let the dealer perform that function.

Once all players have made their decision, going clockwise from the dealer's left all the way around the table to the "third base" position, the seat at the dealer's extreme right, play will move on to the next round.

The Player's Second Option

After all player's have made their decisions on bet circle "1", the dealer now turns over one of the two community cards in front of him so that each player knows four of the five cards that will be used to form his or her final hand.

Again, just like in the first round, players are faced with the decision to let their bet in circle "2" ride, or to take it down and put it back into their bankroll. The motions are the same. Players wishing to let their wager ride slide their cards under their bet in circle "2". And those wishing to remove their bets, scrape the table with their cards. Players that elect to remove their bet in circle "2" from play will have it returned to them by the dealer.

All players may remove their second bet, the one in circle "2", even players that chose to let the bet in circle "1" ride. Each bet is independent of the previous bet. For example, one player may remove the bet in circle 1 and let the bet in circle 2 ride; another may Let it Ride in circle 1 but remove it in circle 2; a third may remove bets in both circles; and a fourth may let both bets ride. All these combinations are permissible.

When all players have completed their playing decisions on their bets in circle "2", it is time for the showdown.

The Showdown

The dealer will now turn over the second and last community card. By combining the two community cards with the player's three individual cards, each player will know his or her final five card hand. All cards are now exposed and each player can see how they fared on this deal.

Unlike the previous two rounds, the bet in circle "3" cannot be removed. This bet is for keeps and will now be settled by the dealer along with any other bets that the players have in the other betting circles, if any.

Going from his right and proceeding to his left, the dealer will turn over each player's cards and settle the wagers.

Settling The Bets

Players who hold at least a pair of 10's or higher ranked poker hand qualify for payouts according to the payout schedule we showed earlier.

Winning hands pay out on all spots which still contain bets. For example, a player holding a pair of Jacks, which pays 1-1, and having $5 bet on each of the three spots, would win $15 total, $5 for each of the spots. Thus $30 would get returned to the player, $15 in winnings plus the original $15 wagered. If only spots 2 and 3 contained $5 bets, then $20 would be returned to the player, $10 in which would be winnings ($5 each on circles 2 and 3).

By the same token, players whose hands didn't qualify for the payoff will lose on all spots where they had bets. At the very least, that would be one losing spot, the third circle whose bet cannot be removed, and at a maximum, three spots if the player let all bets ride. Thus, if a player bet $5, and let all bets ride, but lost, then $15 would be lost, $5 on each circle. However, if the player had removed the bets from circles 1 and 2, then only $5 would be lost.

Let's now see how the other wagers work, the $1 Progressive bet, which is being phased out, and the new Bonus Bet.

$1 BONUS OR TOURNAMENT BET

Players have the option to make a separate $1 bet which will go toward an additional payout pool. There will be a Tournament or Bonus spot on the table to accommodate this wager, and it is made before the cards are dealt by placing $1 in the circle marked for this wager.

Formerly, this $1 bet allowed players to earn entry into the big money Let it Ride Tournament if the player drew a straight flush or royal flush hand. Beginning October 1, 1997, the tournament began to be phased out, and was replaced by a new version called the Let it Ride Bonus.

The new Let it Ride Bonus $1 side bet was introduced in October 1, 1997, to replace the $1 Tournament side wager in the Let it Ride table games. Almost all games now feature the Bonus Bet, however, there still are a few casinos still running the Tournament.

We'll look at both of these individually, beginning with the Let it Ride Bonus wager.

LET IT RIDE BONUS

The Bonus wager works similar to the previous Tournament – a $1 bet is placed in the betting circle before the cards are drawn and winners are determined according to the hand that is drawn.

Where the two games differ is that the Bonus payout is fixed according to a set schedule and is paid out on the spot: there are no tournament playoffs as before, and no million dollar bounty waiting for the one lucky winner who goes all the way and wins the tournament.

However, this new Bonus paytable is actually much better for the average player. Rather than building a large pool of money that gets distributed to the few, the million dollar payouts are now circulated back into the regular paytables and get distributed among many. This concept is similar to progressive slot machines. The super jackpot machines pay less out to the regular players as money is saved for the jackpot winner, while the smaller progressives keep the money flowing.

As of the time of this writing, there were twenty-four bonus paytables in effect for winners of the Let it Ride Bonus. The paytables used in a particular jurisdiction are determined by the local gaming commissions. Some areas allow just one paytable, while others approve multiple paytables that may be used. In the latter case, it is up to the casino management as to which paytable they will offer their patrons.

There is a wide range of pay schedules among these machines. Payouts for the best hand, the royal flush, range from $25,000 to $10,000; full houses can range anywhere from $75 to $200, and right on down to all the other winning hands.

Another differences occurs in the paytables as well. While some paytables give bonuses for hands as weak as a high pair (10's or better), others start paying out for two pair hands. Other games require a minimum strength of three of a kind.

The amounts that a casino pays on these wagers directly affect a players overall return on the money gambled, and of course, the house edge on the bet. With the most liberal payouts allowed, the player will buck a 3.05% house edge on the Bonus bet. The least liberal, can give the casino an edge as high as

35% or more, depending on the other payouts, steep odds for a casino bet.

Keep in mind that it is not necessarily how easy it is to get a payout on a hand that determines your overall chances of winning, but the amounts that will get paid on all winning hands overall. For example, just because one paytable makes 10's or better hands a winning combination, does not mean it has overall better odds than a paytable that pays with a minimum hand of a three of a kind.

The first three schedules, A, B, and C, show the most common payouts found.

LET IT RIDE $1 BONUS PAYOUT SCHEDULE A

Royal Flush	$20,000
Straight Flush	$2,000
Four of a Kind	$200
Full House	$75
Flush	$50
Straight	$25
Three of a Kind	$5
Two Pairs	$4
10's or Better	$1

Following is the second of the common Let it Ride Bonus paytables in use.

LET IT RIDE $1 BONUS PAYOUT SCHEDULE B

Royal Flush	$20,000
Straight Flush	$2,000
Four of a Kind	$100
Full House	$75
Flush	$50
Straight	$25
Three of a Kind	$9
Two Pairs	$6
10's or Better	No Payout

Following is the third of the common Let it Ride Bonus paytables in use.

LET IT RIDE $1 BONUS PAYOUT SCHEDULE C

Royal Flush	$20,000
Straight Flush	$2,000
Four of a Kind	$400
Full House	$200
Flush	$50
Straight	$25
Three of a Kind	$5
Two Pairs	No Payout
10's or Better	No Payout

As we see, each of the common paytables we've shown follow a different philosophy. Schedule A, for example, stresses frequent winners, Schedule C emphasizes less frequent winners (two pair and tens or better do not pay) with larger payouts on the three of a kind, full house, and four of a kind hands, while Schedule B mixes the two philosophies in a different blend.

LET IT RIDE TOURNAMENT BET

Let it Ride's initial marketing push and game rules featured the $1 side bet being applied to the Let it Ride Tournament, an exciting concept which saw eligible straight flush and royal flush winners being invited to a special playoff tournament with big prizes for the winners. The rules originally allowed only 50 players to qualify for the tournament, which meant players had to have at least a straight flush of 8 or better, and as the tournament grew in popularity, it was expanded to 100 players, and then more. In 1997, four million dollars was handed out in cash for tournament winners.

However, the tournament is almost completely phased out, replaced by the Bonus game we discussed earlier. We will discuss the tournament here in case it is brought back or the player finds a rare game still offering the tournament. We suspect however, that by the year 2000, the tournament games will become a thing of the past, unless the Shuffle Master company decides to reinstate the tournament at a later date.

While the million dollar jackpot possibilities of the $1 Tournament are the big draw of this bet, there is an additional attraction to this wager - the $1 tournament bet also qualifies the player for cash bonuses if a straight or better hand is drawn. The following chart shows these bonus payouts.

LET IT RIDE
$1 TOURNAMENT PAYOUT/BONUS PAYOUTS

Royal Flush	$20,000
Straight Flush	$2,000
Four of a Kind	$200
Full House	$75
Flush	$50
Straight	$20

The tournament bet is made by placing $1 on the red button located in front of the three betting spots. Note that while a pair of tens or higher pair, two pair, and three of a kind hands will win on the regular betting circles, they don't qualify for the bonus payouts on the $1 bet. The minimum bonus payout for this bet, as we see on the chart, is a straight or better.

We'll go over a sample bonus win for both the three betting circles and the $1 Tournament bet to make the payoffs in Let it Ride perfectly clear.

Let's say the player had $5 bet, let the bets ride in all three betting spots, and drew a flush for his five cards. Each of the three betting circles would receive an 8-1 payoff (for the flush) on the $5 bet, for a $40 win per circle, or $120 total on those bets. Of course, if only one bet circle contained a bet, that win would be only $40. In addition to this win, the player earns $50 for the bonus payout on the $1 tournament bet. Thus, the total win for that round would be $120 plus $50, for a grand total of $170.

If that hand was instead a straight flush, the picture would be a whole lot sweeter. Each spot now would win $1,000 (the $5 bet at 200-1) for a total of $3,000 on the three spots, plus the bonus win of $2,000 for a grand total win of $5,000. And the really good news is that the player would automatically get entered into Let it Ride, The Tournament, where $1,000,000 could be won!

However, to receive the bonus payouts and possible entry into the tournament, the player must have made that $1 tournament wager.

Let It Ride – The Tournament

The Let it Ride Tournament allows participating players the chance to win a million dollar jackpot or higher. The tournament was set up so that there were four qualifying rounds a year, each one lasting for a period of three months. These exciting and lucrative events are only open to players who paid the $1 "entry fee" and were lucky enough to hit a straight or royal flush on that hand.

All players who receive a straight flush or royal flush during the three month qualifying period (and who had the $1 bet on the red button for the tournament bet) will be asked to fill out a tournament registration form at the time of winning. When the three month qualifying period is up, these players will be invited by the Shuffle Master Corporation to participate in the Tournament Playoffs.

And here is where the really big money can be won. At the very minimum, participants get guaranteed cash prizes beginning at $1,000. And for the lucky player who goes all the way, the grand prize of one million dollars will be the reward.

There are four rounds in the playoffs. Each player in this first qualifying round, as in every succeeding round, is given an equal amount of chips to start. Players are pitted against each other with the goal of trying to win more chips than their opponents so they can move on to the following rounds. These chips have no cash value and are only used for the purpose of determining winners on a round by round basis.

The first round gives each player a guaranteed $1,000 bonus just for playing. The top 100 winners in this first round will move on to the second round and receive an additional $1,000 bonus for their efforts, while the losers will have to settle for their original $1,000 and their "what ifs."

In this second round, players start fresh again with an equal amount of non-redeemable chips. No winnings are carried over from round one. Again, players make their best efforts to build up the winnings, hoping to be among the top winners so they can move on once again, one step closer to the million dollar grand prize.

Only the top 25 players from round two move on to round three, accompanied by another $1,000 bonus. These 25 players have now earned $3,000 in prizes, but their sights are set on going one more round, to round four where the big money prizes await. Again, chips are divided up with an equal number going to the 25 competitors.

When the dust settles, it will be only the top six players who move on to the fourth and final round and the big prizes. These six players now play for the banana split with all the fixings - three scoops, two toppings, whip cream, sprinkles, and a cherry.

WINNING AT LET IT RIDE

In this final round, players are playing for a one million dollar prize! While the losers may be disappointed in not coming in first, they don't do too shabby either - there are $450,000 in prizes for the runners-up.

The prize schedule for the top six finalists is shown below.

FINISH	TOURNAMENT PRIZE
1st	$1,000,000
2nd	$200,000
3rd	$100,000
4th	$75,000
5th	$50,000
6th	$25,000

THE WINNING STRATEGIES

In this section, we'll go over the third and fourth card playing strategies for Let it Ride, the house percentages inherent to the game, and the overall strategy for winning at Let it Ride.

The main strategy considerations in Let it Ride center around the bets that have been made in the first two betting circles, 1 and 2, where the player has a choice of letting these bets ride or bringing them down and playing only for the mandatory bet in the third circle. Thus, there are two decisions to make, one for each circle.

The first decision occurs when we've looked at our three cards and decide on letting the bet ride in circle 1 or bringing it down. We'll call this the Three Card Betting Strategy. The second decision occurs when the dealer has exposed a community card, the player's fourth known card, and we must now decide the fate of the bet in circle 2. Since this occurs when we have knowledge of four of our cards, we'll call this the Fourth Card Playing Strategy.

We'll start our strategy discussions with the third card playing strategy.

Third Card Betting Strategy

Our first three cards give us a good indication of where the hand may be headed. We already know three fifths of the cards that will comprise our final hand and can make a clear determination on the best way to play the bets.

Sometimes, as in the case of three of a kind or a pair of tens or better, the strategy decision is obvious - we're already sitting with winners and should let the bet ride. A payout is already guaranteed and with a little luck, that hand may improve to a stronger rank and larger payoff. We'll also play strong hands that don't yet have a guaranteed payoff but which give us a positive expectation of winning.

On the other side of the coin, weak hands with negative expectations of winning will dictate a strategy of minimizing losses and the correct play will be to take down the bet in circle 1.

Below are the seven categories of Let it Ride poker hands where the optimal play is to let the bet ride in circle 1. Hands are listed from the strongest to the weakest. The reader is reminded that 10's, J's, Q's, K's, and A's, are considered high cards, cards that if paired will payoff as a winner.

Hands that We Will Play

We'll let our bet ride with the following three card hands:

1. Three of a Kind

This is fairly obvious. We've got an automatic winner guaranteeing us at least a 3-1 payoff on all our bet spots.

2. Pair of 10's or Higher Pair

Another obvious play. We already have a 1-1 payoff, and can't lose. Improving the hand will give us an even larger payout.

3. Three to a Royal Flush

We have all sorts of shots here for a payoff; a flush, a straight, a high pair (and even three of a kind and two pair), and of course, the hand we would really like to get, a Royal Flush.

4. Three to a Straight Flush

Ditto above. There are good possibilities for improvement. We should let the bet ride.

5. Three to a Flush with Two Cards 10 or Higher and a Straight Possibility

It is not enough to have the flush chance, for there are two additional suited cards that must be matched up. We must also have the value of the two high cards, which can pair, and the possibility of the straight. The combination of all the above factors make this hand a profitable one to let the bet ride. An example of this hand is Q J 9 of clubs, or K J 9 of hearts.

6. Three to a Flush with J 9 8, 10 9 7 or 10 8 7

Unlike the above grouping, which can be played with a two gap straight possibility, these three hands have only one high card and are thus more marginal as a playable combination. They need the greater straight possibilities of the one gap hand (compared to the two gap straight in category 5) to make letting the bet ride a profitable play. These hands can also be thought of as a three card flush with one high card and one gap.

7. 10 J Q or J Q K

These hands, the most marginal of the seven categories, but still profitable enough to let the bet ride, provide two good possibilities for payoffs. First, any of the three cards, if paired, gives us a payoff with the added outside chance of trips on the fifth card; and second, both hands are open-ended straight possibilities that can fill into a winner paying 5-1.

Hands that We Won't Play

Unless you have one of the hands in the seven categories listed in the above section, you should remove your bet from the first circle. While there are always winning possibilities with any three starting cards, the cost of playing low percentage hands is too costly to justify letting the bet ride.

Where you have a chance to remove a bet with inferior cards, you should always do so. That's the smart way to play.

Let's now move on to the strategy for the next round.

Fourth Card Betting Strategy

After the dealer exposes one of the two community downcards, each player knows four of the five cards that will make up his or her final hand. We're faced with our final strategy decision: Should we let our bet ride, or should we reclaim it back into our bankroll?

As with the third card betting strategy, we'll play hands that give us a positive expectation of winning, and take down our bet in the second circle when our expectation of winning is negative. In the obvious cases where we already have a winning combination, the clear-cut play of course, is to let the bet ride. However, in many cases, we won't be quite as thrilled with our prospects, and would like nothing better than to take down our bet with our lousy cards.

Below, we'll look at the full strategy for letting bets ride or taking them down on circle 2.

Hands that We Will Play

We'll let our bet ride with the following four card hands.

1. Four of a Kind

This is an obvious winning hand paying 50-1. Let 'em ride!

2. Three or a Kind

This is also an obvious winner, paying 3-1 on all betting circles. Let 'em ride!

3. Two Pair - A clear-cut play

We already have a guaranteed 2-1 payoff with possibilities of improving to a full house for an 11-1 yield.

4. Pair of 10's or Higher Pair

We've already got a winner paying 1-1 and can improve to a two pair or three of a kind hand with a good draw on the final card.

5. Four to a Royal Flush

One more card, and we're there with a big payoff. There are also the possibilities of making a flush or straight, and an excellent chance of catching a high paying pair since any of our four high cards, if matched, becomes a winner.

6. Four to a Straight Flush

This is not as strong as a four to a royal flush, but it is still holds excellent possibilities.

7. Four to a Flush

The payoff of 8-1 should the flush be drawn is greater than the odds of filling the flush, and is therefore an excellent bet. Of the 48 unseen cards in the deck, nine of them will make the flush, and 39 will not, odds of 4.33-1. Being paid 8-1 on odds of about 4.33-1 is always a great bet in my book.

8. Four to an Open-Ended Straight

When there are no high cards held, this bet is a wash. Of the 48 unseen cards, eight of them will make the straight, and 40 will not, odds of 5-1. Since the payoff is exactly 5-1, we have an even chance - there is no theoretical loss or gain on the play. We could choose to let our bet ride, or take it down.

If there is at least one high card as part of the open-ended straight, we now gain the advantage on the four card open ended straight draw, for the last community card may pair with our high card for a winner.

9. Four to a High Straight

The hands 10-J-Q-A, 10-Q-K-A, 10-J-K-A, and J-Q-K-A, have two things in common; the ability to match any of the four high cards into a paying winner, and the possibilities of filling to an inside straight. Neither factor by itself is enough to make the third bet, but together, due to the sensitivity of the single deck game, form enough strength to let the third bet ride, though marginally.

Hands that We Won't Play

Lacking any of the nine combinations listed above, in other words, holding hands of various degrees of junk, gives us a negative expectation on this fourth card and the strategy is clear - take down the bet and have it returned to your bankroll.

THE NEW MODELS

In the new versions of the Let it Ride video machines, which will be delivered on the IGT video slots platform, Shuffle Master has made some changes that they hope will spur interest in their revamped versions. As we go to press, some of their plans with the new machines are as yet unclear and await testing in the casinos, but we've managed to obtain some preliminary plans about the nature of the new configurations.

Two important changes will probably be incorporated into the new designs.

First of all, to simplify the game and give regular players a good return, the biggest change will be to eliminate the $1 bonus bet. The new Let it Ride video games will feature only the basic paytable.

The second important change will be to reduce the maximum allowed bet from five units to three units on each of the betting circles. Thus, a player would insert nine coins maximum to play the video machine, three coins on each of the betting circles available.

So overall, where the old machines took a total of 16 coins, five on each betting circle and the bonus bet, the new ones hit the player for only nine coins total. That's a substantial amount less for players to put at risk, and should reduce overall losses for the players.

Less losses means more winners, which for players, translates to more play for the buck.

At the time of this writing, Shuffle Master had not yet decided on the paytables they would offer the players, but my sources there indicated that they were going to offer players a reasonable shake to induce play. Their biggest challenge, they said, was to reduce the risk of exposure for players that didn't know how to play, so that they could keep these players interested.

The company will go through a testing period and offer various paytables in different venues to see which ones generate the most interest. While they have offered some excellent payoff schedules, at the same time, there have been some largely unfavorable ones as well, so we'll have to see what holds in the marketplace.

Winning Strategies

The strategies on the new machines will be identical to the table games if the same winning hands are required for a payoff. However, if that is not the case, you will need to adjust your strategies according to the paytable itself.

For example, on some of the machines, a minimum hand of eights or better might qualify for a payoff. If this is the actual payoff on the machine you're playing, you would have to adjust your thinking to incorporate eights and nines as high cards. These cards, of course, would be in addition to the tens or better. If nines or sevens are used, you'll need to adjust accordingly as well.

Below, we'll just highlight a few basic ideas to keep in mind for playing strategy.

Third Card Betting Strategy

As in the table version, we automatically let the bets ride for any hands that offer an automatic payout. There is nothing to lose in these situations. At a minimum, there is a paying winner, and if there is a lucky draw, a bigger winner.

We'll also play strong hands that don't yet have a guaranteed payoff but which have a positive winning expectation. Similarly, with poor cards, we always want to use the unique feature of the game that allows us to remove our bet from the table

If you have pairs less than 8's, one way straights, and any weak hands, you should remove your bet from the first circle. The cost of playing low percentage hands is too costly to justify letting the bet ride.

Fourth Card Betting Strategy

When we already have a winning hand, the obvious strategy is to let the bet ride. We'll also let our bets ride with very good straight, flush, straight flush, and royal flush possibilities.

By the same token, bets should be taken down when the cards held have no winners or little future of winning. Actually, we'll only let the bet ride when our hand gives us an outright advantage.

With none of the solid combinations that are automatic winners or show great promise, take down the last bet. Do not be tempted to play weak hands in the hopes that your weak four card hand can improve to a winner on a lucky draw. That will happen sometimes, but the problem is that you'll lose money in the long run trying to squeeze a few winners out of poor starting cards.

HOUSE PERCENTAGES

The best percentage that can be achieved at the Let it Ride table games is about 3.5% against the player for the basic bets. This is assuming that the player uses the optimal basic strategy we present here and that the $1 bet is not made on the tournament or bonus bet spots.

Less than optimal play at the table can cost the player multiple percentage points, the severity of which depends on the number of mistakes or poor decisions made. The more of an edge the player gives the house, on average, the more money that player will lose when he or she plays.

For example, a player who doesn't let his bets ride on automatic winning hands or who lets his bets ride on terrible starting cards, will increase the house edge precipitously.

Players who make bets on the optional $1 tournament or bonus spot are giving the casino a much larger edge, an edge that varies depending upon the payouts for the particular casino played in.

Making poor percentage bets will raise the overall house edge higher than the 3.5% stated here.

The smaller the average bet, the higher that house percentage would be. For example, a poor percentage $1 bet has a greater overall negative effect on an average $5 bettor than an average $25 bettor.

In the video versions of Let it Ride, the player may find better chances of winning due to a more aggressive payout schedule. This was the case with some early machines, but there was also versions that put the player at a less than desirable disadvantage. Keep in mind that the frequency of play is so much greater on a video machine than a table game, that every percentage point disadvantage the player faces at a Let it Ride video machine is magnified and will show up as bigger losses.

For example, at a table game, a player may get dealt about 50-60 hands per hour, more if there is just one player gambling there. But at a machine, a super fast player can get in as many as 600 plays per hour, while an average player can do perhaps 300-500 plays.

While the Shuffle Master organization is still experimenting with the exact form of machine they will be offering customers, a simple check of the payout schedule may give you a good idea as to whether you're getting a better game or not.

ODDS OF DRAWING HANDS

Following is a table showing the odds of getting dealt winning hands in Let it Ride. These are the same odds as those in regular draw poker (first five cards dealt) and Caribbean Stud Poker.

ODDS OF DRAWING WINNING HANDS	
Royal Flush	649,739 -1
Straight Flush	72,192 -1
Four of a Kind	4,165 -1
Full House	693 -1
Flush	508 -1
Straight	254 -1
Three of a Kind	46 -1
Two Pair	20 -1
One Pair	1.37 -1

More Percentages of Play

In Let it Ride, most starting hands have losing expectations for the player. In fact, in 85 out of 100 hands (actually 84.5%), the correct playing strategy dictates that both the first and second bets would be removed, and that only the third bet, the one that cannot be removed, be played. It is the other 15% of the time, where the player's hand is in an advantageous situation, that more money is wagered in the form of letting the second or third bets ride.

We take advantage of these profitable situations by making sure money is bet on our hand. It is on these occasions, particularly when all three bets are riding, where the larger losses of the 85% of the hands that are dealt to a losing expectation are made up by betting more in a winning situation. Those second and third bets are where we make up lost ground. Like any good gambling strategy, the general rule is to minimize losses and maximize gains.

Using the proper playing strategy, a total of two bets will stay in action about 8.5% of the time, and the full three bets, 7.0% of the time.

When all three situations are added up, the wagers with one bet, the wagers with two bets and the wagers with three bets, the house edge will emerge at 3.5% at the table version of Let it Ride if our playing strategy is followed.

Frequency of Wins

To get a winning payout of any kind will occur about one hand in four, 23.88% at the time, at either of the two basic Let it Ride paytables. On the Bonus paytables, the frequency of winning will range up to 23.88% if the same number of payoffs are given, and less, of course, when there are fewer payoffs to be had.

The video version of Let it Ride that offers payouts on eights or better, gives the player a frequency at winning of about three times in ten, or 30.38% to be exact. If the machines offer payouts for hands of tens or better, then these video units, of course, would have the same 23.88% frequency of winning as the table game.

STRATEGY OVERVIEW

The 3.5% house edge in the Let it Ride basic table game on the three bet circles is higher than the overall 2.56% of Caribbean Stud Poker when the call and ante bets are combined, and other table games such as blackjack, baccarat and craps, when those games are played properly. It is also higher than single zero roulette, which is starting to become more prevalent in U.S. casinos.

The big draw for the original versions of Let it Ride was the $1 tournament bet and the hope of hitting a monster hand. However, this wager is much worse than the 3.5% edge of the basic game, and the new Bonus game, with that same $1 bet depending upon the payout schedule offered, can be poor as well.

I personally don't like making high percentage negative bets, and if I do, I might be more apt to go for the multi-millions of the lottery with that same $1 bet. But then again, as opposed to the lottery, Let it Ride lets players participate in the action, make decisions that effect the outcome of the game, and of course, can be part of the casino experience.

It is my recommendation that players who want the best odds possible at Let it Ride stay away from the $1 tournament or bonus bets due to the typical poor odds of these wagers, but of course, other considerations must be taken in as well.

The overall attraction of the extra bonus bet is that it gives players a chance to win large sums of money with just a $1 wager. Again, making a comparison with the lottery, while these bets may not have the glamour of the million dollar jackpot offered by lottery games, they do offer odds that are worlds better than the lottery hustles.

And with much better chances of winning something good for just a little money, the Let it Ride bonus bet has become popular among players. And since fun is what gambling is supposed to be about, if you don't mind the steeper odds, at least you have a much better shot at winning something here than throwing a buck away on the numbers game.

315

Baccarat Master Card Counter
NEW WINNING STRATEGY!

For the **first time**, Gambling Research Institute releases the **latest winning techniques** at baccarat. This **exciting** strategy, played by big money players in Monte Carlo and other exclusive locations, is based on principles that have made insiders and pros **hundreds of thousands of dollars** counting cards at blackjack - card counting!

NEW WINNING APPROACH

This brand **new** strategy now applies card counting to baccarat to give you a **new winning approach,** and is designed so that any player, with just a little effort, can successfully take on the casinos at their own game - and win!

SIMPLE TO USE, EASY TO MASTER

You learn how to count cards for baccarat without the mental effort needed for blackjack! No need to memorize numbers - keep the count on the scorepad. Easy-to-use, play the strategy while enjoying the game!

LEARN WHEN TO BET BANKER, WHEN TO BET PLAYER

No longer will you make bets on hunches and guesses - use the GRI Baccarat Master Card Counter to determine when to bet Player and when to bet Banker. You learn the basic counts (running and true), deck favorability, when to increase bets and much more in this **winning strategy**.

LEARN TO WIN IN JUST ONE SITTING

That's right! After **just one sitting** you'll be able to successfully learn this powerhouse strategy and use it to your advantage at the baccarat table. Be the best baccarat player at the table - the one playing the odds to **win**! Baccarat can be beaten. The Master Card Counter shows you how!

FREE BONUS!

Order now to receive **absolutely free**, The Basics of Winning Baccarat. One quick reading with this great primer shows you how to play and win.

To order, send $50 by bank check or money order to:

Cardoza Publishing.P.O. Box 1500, Cooper Station, New York, NY 10276

WIN MONEY AT BACCARAT!

I want to learn the latest winning techniques at baccarat. Please rush me the **GRI Baccarat Master Card Counter** and **Free Bonus**. Enclosed is a check or money order for $50 (plus postage and handling) to:

Cardoza Publishing

P.O. Box 1500, Cooper Station, New York, NY 10276

Call Toll-Free in U.S. & Canada, 1-800-577-WINS; or fax 718-743-8284

Include $5 ship for U.S; $10 for Canada/Mexico; HI, AK, other countries 4x. Orders outside U.S., money order payable in U.S. dollars on U.S. bank only.

NAME _____

ADDRESS _____

CITY _____ STATE _____ ZIP _____

Order Now! - 30 Day Money Back Guarantee! WinCasPlay

CARDOZA SCHOOL OF BLACKJACK
- Home Instruction Course - $200 OFF! -

At last, after years of secrecy, the **previously unreleased** lesson plans, strategies and playing tactics formerly available only to members of the Cardoza School of Blackjack are now available - and at substantial savings. **Now**, you can **learn at home,** and at your own convenience. Like the full course given at the school, the home instruction course goes **step-by-step** over the winning concepts. We'll take you from layman to **pro**.

MASTER BLACKJACK - Learn what it takes to be a **master player**. Be a **powerhouse**, play with confidence, impunity, and **with the odds** on your side. Learn to be a **big winner** at blackjack.

MAXIMIZE WINNING SESSIONS - You'll **learn how** to take a good winning session and make a **blockbuster** out of it, but just as important, you'll learn to cut your losses. Learn exactly when to end a session. We cover everything from the psychological and emotional aspects of play to altered playing conditions (through the **eye of profitability**) to protection of big wins. The advice here could be worth **hundreds (or thousands) of dollars** in one session alone. Take our guidelines seriously.

ADVANCED STRATEGIES - You'll learn the **latest** in advanced winning strategies. Learn about the **ten-factor**, the **Ace-factor**, the effects of rules variations, how to protect against dealer blackjacks, the winning strategies for single and multiple deck games and how each affects you; you'll learn the **true count**, the multiple deck true count variations, and much, much more.

And, of course, you receive the full Base Count Strategy package.

$200 OFF - LIMITED OFFER - The Cardoza School of Blackjack home instruction course, a $295 retail value (or $895 if taken at the school) is available now for just $95!!!

BONUS! - **Rush** your order in **now** for we're also including, **absolutely free,** the 1,000 word essays, "How to Disguise the Fact that You're an Expert", and "How Not to Get Barred". Among other **inside information** contained here, you'll learn about the psychology of pit bosses and how they spot counters.

To order, send $95 by check or money order to <u>Cardoza Publishing</u>:

SAVE $200 (regular $295 - Only $95 with coupon)

Order Now! Please **rush** me the **Cardoza School of BJ Home instruction Course.** Enclosed is a check or money order for $95 (plus postage) to :

Cardoza Publishing
P.O. Box 1500, Cooper Station, New York, NY 10276

Call Toll-Free in U.S. & Canada, 1-800-577-WINS; or fax 718-743-8284

Include $5 ship for U.S; $10 for Canada/Mexico; HI, AK, other countries 4x. Orders outside U.S., money order payable in U.S. dollars on U.S. bank only.

NAME _____

ADDRESS _____

CITY _____ STATE _____ ZIP _____

Order Now! - 30 Day Money Back Guarantee!

WinCasPlay
